DATE			
NOV 2 '92			
NOV 20 '9.			
FEB 20 '03			
MAR 26 '88			
JUL 0 5 2000			
NOV 1 2 2009			
NOV 2 1 2009			

© THE BAKER & TAYLOR CO

JOGGING: THE DANCE OF DEATH

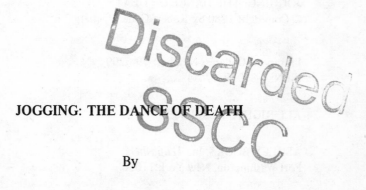

JOGGING: THE DANCE OF DEATH

By

Robert Gene Fineberg

shley Books, Inc.
Port Washington, N. Y. 11050

JOGGING: THE DANCE OF DEATH
© Copyright 1980 by Robert Gene Fineberg

Library of Congress Number: 79-6209
ISBN: 0-87949-174-4

ASHLEY BOOKS, Inc./*Publishers*
Port Washington, New York 11050

Printed in the United States of America
First Edition

9 8 7 6 5 4 3 2 1

Library of Congress Cataloging in Publication Data:

FINEBERG, ROBERT GENE   1940–
    Jogging: The dance of death.

    Includes bibliographical references.
    1. Jogging. 2. Running. 3. Jogging — Accidents
and injuries. 4. Running — Accidents and injuries.
I. Title.
GV494.F56   617'.1027   79-6209
ISBN 0-87949-174-4

"Because they're there . . . "

Anonymous runner answering the question
of why he runs marathons.

Q. What is the warmest temperature you have
ever run in during a workout?

A. One hundred and fifteen degrees with an
ice pack on my head.

From a runner's survey questionnaire.

"The pain at the end was devastating. I
thought I'd die during those last miles.
It was a delicious experience."

Anonymous runner after his first marathon.

i

CONTENTS

FOREWORD

"He's icy cold and not responding," the nurse said. "You'd better see this one real quick." A twenty-five-year-old man had just collapsed at the Portland Marathon. A witness explained that the runner had dropped in his tracks at about the twenty-second mile. It was very cold and damp — a generally disagreeable November afternoon in Oregon.

The race officials had covered the unconscious runner with coats until an ambulance arrived to transport him to the hospital. During the drive he was given enough glucose to arouse a comatose diabetic suffering from an overdose of insulin. The runner didn't respond. Indeed, it was a full twenty minutes later, after his hypothermic body was warmed with heating pads, that he finally began to stir. He was also given additional fluids and glucose.

He could have died. If he had been running alone somewhere, collapsed, and not been given emergency treatment, he would have died from the cold and lowered blood sugar. He was one of the lucky ones who come away from a near-tragedy to compete again.

What happened? No one can say for sure, but at the time the runner arrived in the emergency room, despite the glucose, his blood sugar level was only about half of what it should have been. When fully alert and able to talk, he told me that he had had no prior illness, or even any warnings to help explain his sudden collapse. He had run in previous marathons and had prepared thoroughly for this one.

He was a casualty of racing, a new phenomenon and one that's growing with the increasing involvement in running that's sweeping this country. If the runner who collapsed at the Portland Marathon had read this book he might have been more aware of the dangers of hypo-thermia. If he had been familiar with what the author has to say about distance competition, he could have *avoided the unscheduled trip to the hospital between the twenty-first and twenty-third mile.*

Here, for the first time, is the dark side of jogging; a careful and critical look at the problems, an opportunity to see beyond the hyperbole of the current running gurus. As a doctor who has seen some of these problems at close range, I can only hope that you'll read this book *before* you become a statistic. I strongly urge you to talk with your family physician *before* embarking on what could be a dangerous commitment to fitness. One casualty is one too many.

Edward J. Weinstein, M.D., Ph.D.
Portland, Oregon.

INTRODUCTION

Right at this moment there's nothing less than a nation-wide love affair going on between runners and writers who are writing fondly about running. There's no great mystery to this affair for it has grown from a chance meeting in some small physical education magazine into a passionate intimacy filling dozens of books. And it has all happened in just ten years.

America has taken running to its bosom, jamming streets, roads and highways with everyone from the gentle jogger moving slowly toward fitness to the running maniac pursuing elusive personal goals of time and distance. But beneath this highly successful fad are some startling and sometimes frightening facts. Important questions on the safety and even desirability of running remain to be answered. There are discouraging statistics on injuries. There are problems with the marathon madness that seems to be gripping the country. And most important of all, the essence of running itself is now in sharp focus: with experienced runners dropping dead in their unusual pursuit of immortality, running's preeminent place in cardiovascular exercise is being carefully examined.

I'm not going to set out to prove that running is dangerous or unhealthy just because it's running. I will stress the need for caution and I will try to show that, like other fads that require careful handling, running *in extremis* can be lethal. It can be the dance of death. And it has been just that for the unwary.

These are the years for running books. There are virtually dozens on the market and most of them glow with the positive attributes of running. Some of the books, unfortunately, praise running to the point of delusion. No exercise, just as no food, no vitamin, or no state of mind, can deliver a long and disease-free life. It's still only *one* component out of many that make up a balanced and healthy lifestyle.

In this book, I'm looking the running community straight in the eye and stating the point directly: running *may not* be all it is cracked up to be!

Who runs and why are the questions posed in the first chapter. The running subculture also comes under magnification here. Certainly the proliferation of runners has been directly related to the people who are making money from the joggers who take to the streets each day. And since there are nearly 25 million of us, the salesmanship is second to none.

The second chapter deals with the myths that exist about running. Can running *really* improve your physical and mental well-being? Is running good for everyone? What about injuries?

Chapter 3 explores the dangers that exist for the jogger on the streets of this country. The hazards that come from sharing space with automobiles are looked at soberly. Muggers and dogs are discussed with an eye to safety. And weather is emphasized as a very important factor that continues to plague the unsuspecting runner.

The fourth chapter covers the injuries that are increasing at an alarming rate. Equipment also comes under fire — especially the expensive shoes that seem to be the hottest item to hit the stores since man first wrapped his bare feet in animal skins, thousands and thousands of years ago.

The ultradistance craze and the frantic marathon in particular are looked at in chapter 5. Distance running *may not be for everyone*. High mileage could very well spell trouble for the neophyte. The taken-for-granted pairing of running and health begins to separate under this exploration.

Chapter 6 takes the full measure of running itself and zeroes in on the *sudden exercise death* (SED) that can't be explained away by the running subculture as just another week-end warrior trying too much, too soon. This expose is long overdue.

The seventh chapter is a full and helpful lexicon of all those terms that can confuse a runner who is reading the dozens of magazines and books that crowd shelves in bookstores everywhere. The terminology is explained in the language we all use in our daily living.

Chapter 8 provides a comprehensive look at these books and magazines. It's a tremendous task keeping up with the literature of running, but this section will enable you to have an understanding of where you are in relation to the information at hand.

This book comes with my personal guarantee: that after reading it, you'll not be so quick to look at running through myopic lenses; you'll see that running is not the "be all and end all." It was Socrates who said, "All things in moderation." This is my message too and my hope is that you'll be a more discerning runner today so that you'll be a healthy and whole runner tomorrow.

Good luck and healthy jogging.

JOGGING: THE DANCE OF DEATH

CHAPTER ONE: THE FRENZY OF FITNESS

"This obsession with running is
really an obsession with the
potential for more and more life."

George A. Sheehan, M.D.
Dr. Sheehan on Running

Running a mile, that old track and field standby, used to be a physical achievement to be very proud of. For many years it was almost the only standard for high school cross-country runners. Any distance beyond a mile was considered fairly dangerous and a near impossibility for the young female runner. Running a couple of miles back to back was too good to be true if you weren't a distance star. If, for example, you were one of those crazy club runners who could spin off six to ten miles in a week-end race, you were part of the ephemeral "track team" that was always composed of people with alleged built-in advantages. "He's got a lot of wind, ya' know."

Sometime during the latter part of the last decade, marathoning, the race of all races, caught on. It's still the "in" part of distance running and an event that can draw as many spectators as an NFL football game. But unlike football, spectators along the marathon route can participate by handing out wet sponges, oranges, and small cups of water. It's a real community happening!

But something has happened to the traditional marathon. The change came about when hard-working marathon regulars, those people who plan their lives and their years around four or five really important distance events, including jaunts to such exotic places as Athens, Greece, and Fukuoka, Japan, wanted something more. They wanted something they could call their own, an event or events that couldn't be packed by beginners hot off a couple of weeks of training, hoping to transverse the 26 miles and 385 yards with luck, sweat, and dogged determination. And making it. The beginners, in other words, were stealing the show from the regulars.

The solution was simple: increase the distance and make running into a constant quest for records. If beginners could stagger, shuffle and jog through a regulation marathon, stage races of 50 miles or more. Add in a 100-mile race and find such out-of-the-way places as Death Valley and Pike's Peak to stage events. There have even been advertisements in a running magazine soliciting support for an attempt to run across the Sahara Desert. There's no end to what is technically possible when the frenzy of fitness dips into the current world atlas. In short, ultra-marathons have now exacerbated the dizzying pace for fitness.

People start to run for many reasons. This seems obvious by just talking with a few runners. There is no real consensus beyond general concepts and there are as many motivations as there are runners. Some of the reasons have little to do with physical fitness and the eternal search for a perfect exercise. Some people run because the challenge of gaining new ground is addictive, almost an instinct. A rabid curiosity overcomes most of us when we stumble on a track with some running event in progress. For example, there are two things we all want to know: how far are they running and what's the record for the event in progress? It's a natural human thirst for the knowledge of what's different.

When someone begins jogging he or she is faced with a couple of critical questions. First, how far should he/she run at any one time? Nobody goes into running with the intention of someday running from Canada to Mexico

13

during a summer vacation. This comes later, much later. This comes when running develops into a passion — more than an exercise!

The second question is: what's to be accomplished on a long-term basis? Most joggers start off by trying to accomplish a very practical goal like losing weight or increasing lung power so that a couple of games of week-end tennis aren't equivalent to trying to scale the Andes. Many runners, however, have a goal that's vague, an amorphous idea linked tenuously to improving health.

That is the way it begins for most joggers. However, something happens along the way that turns gentle jogging, a term coined by the running subculture to mean the easy shuffling pace geared to cover many miles slowly, into a frenzy of activity, culminating in such unbelievable events as the twenty-four-hour run and the twenty-four-hour marathon relay.[1]

What is it that eventually goes off in a runner's head and turns him from a smooth-striding, smiling, sweat-covered fun-runner into a violent-stepping, determined, blood-caked ultramarathoner? What makes an ultramarathoner out of a neighborhood jogger?

Most runners will admit that they run to keep in shape, to maintain physical fitness. If this is true, and it is for some, why do most runners run so many more miles than is really necessary for fitness? Does a marathon help you feel better when you're virtually unconscious on your feet at the end? Other runners claim that they run to improve stamina and endurance. Does this include running until the stamina and endurance are drained away by too many miles in too short a time span? Some, according to what has been written before, run for peace of mind: to feel better emotionally, to remove tension and make life's daily exasperations more tolerable. Does this mean running with a vengeance, feeling that skipping a day or two is almost like committing a sin?[2]

Running seems to grow on most serious runners like the gambling casino grows on the serious gambler. There's a psychological reward to running, a pay-off that can't be measured on treadmills or by stopwatches, a pay-off that is at once highly personal to each participant and yet common enough that a collective pattern grows into a community consciousness. Running grows on the newcomer so quickly that sometimes it is literally overnight that the beginner takes to competition and the attractions associated with distance running. It can happen so fast, yet the consequences can be devastating.

The frenzy of fitness becomes the challenge for existence itself. Running becomes living and vice versa. The runner grows into a new awareness that here on the streets of his neighborhood is the ultimate in survival at a price he can definitely afford.

15

No one in his right mind would decide, after passing the age of forty, to challenge football on a professional level. It would be considered foolhardy. You can, however, challenge a marathon at that age (or beyond) and even have your own category so that all the prizes don't go to the youthful runners. Nobody would think twice about competitive soccer after passing their prime physically. But you can run in an all-comers track meet and come home with a ribbon, certificate or tee-shirt for your courage. No sensible baseball player, beginning to face the inevitable decline in his athletic performance, would look to the World Series as a chance to capture glory. You can, however, run in the world series of running – the Boston Marathon – simply by finishing a prior recognized marathon in a minimum qualifying time (2 hours and 40 minutes for men under forty years of age; 3 hours and 10 minutes for men over forty and women). In fact, if that's still too much to ask, you can run unofficially by just showing up and staying at the rear of the massive mob waiting for the starter's gun to signal the hours of physical and mental torture.

The challenge of running becomes intensely personal, even to the point of testing oneself against oneself. Running can become a one-on-one contest where you are both offensive and defensive at the same time. After competing in the 1977 Palos Verdes Marathon, the *Los Angeles Herald*

Examiner's Chic Perkins wrote, "To me (and I know I speak for everyone in this regard), it was a tingling sense of pride having accomplished a truly exceptional feat. So what if 468 people finished ahead of me? I still finished and that's all that matters. I may never walk again, but why worry about a trivial thing like that?"[3]

Jim Caulfield of Los Angeles specializes in testing himself. He has run 92 miles from Santa Barbara to Los Angeles on behalf of the Jerry Lewis Muscular Dystrophy Telethon, as well as a 45-miler on behalf of the Guatemalan earthquake fund. He's also been in a 100-mile run for the USO. Is Jim Caulfield unique? Not too many of his caliber, right? Wrong. There are hundreds of runners who have set out on extremely long distances to test themselves against themselves. Stunts are stunts, but stunts with the goal of survival create something of a religious fervor that can't be summarily dismissed by nonrunners.

Actor Bruce Dern, for example, a runner of some experience and seasoning, has run from Furnace Creeek in Death Valley, to Stove Pipe Wells, a distance of twenty-four miles. Less than a marathon perhaps, but he ran it in Death Valley's midsummer, with temperatures hovering around 115 degrees!

Diana Nyad, a distance swimmer with a reputation for tackling the difficult after the impossible, runs twelve miles every day at a respectable six minutes per mile pace.

"Sure I get nauseous and vomit and ache," she told writer Nancy Spiller for *Outside* magazine in 1978, "but I do the same in swimming. If you're in great shape and can push past certain pain barriers, then running is a great playground for that sort of thing."

Author Joseph Wambaugh also talked with Nancy Spiller. He said that running is not a social event. "I am in such torment, crying out for the sins of man — I run alone."

Pain, physical as well as mental, continues for all runners caught up in the desire for ever more mileage and ever more speed. It continues for those with the drive to cover distances great enough to be considered personal challenges. A Mt. Everest of one's own looms every time a dedicated runner takes to the streets looking for more and more competition.

So why do these runners run? Because it's there, as Sir Edmund Hillary said when asked why he climbed mountains. *What's there* when it comes to running? The dark at the edge of the soul. That black hole that all of us walk close to but rarely cross over. It's failure against success. It's beating the odds. It's doing what some say can't be done. It's mind against body for supremacy; spirit versus the flesh. The eternal quest for the separation of man from animal and a closer relationship with the gods we gave up millenia ago. It's something that seems worthwhile against nothing that seems worthwhile. It's

18

what Jose Ortega y Gasset in *Revolt of the Masses* said is the precipice of life; that edge that all of us have to walk perilously close to our entire lives. The Spanish philosopher zeroed in on the condition of man when he wrote that it's up to each of us to keep from falling off that precipice of life.

How does the frenzy of running enter the philosophical picture? Ortega's precipice of life is most clearly seen near the end of a marathon. It's that period when everything the runner is — every tendon, every nerve cell, every muscle in the body — screams to quit, to allow the immediate luxury of stepping off that precipice Ortega outlines. But allowing the agony to end, the pain to stop, is merely a false luxury, however, for when the physical agony ends, the mental agony begins. And the cause of the agony is failure, failure to transcend the physical, failure to conquer the weaker link. This, then, is the running precipice that is walked, stepped, jogged and finally run by in distance running. Balancing on the edge of the running precipice and *not stepping off* is a heady experience. If you watch runners finishing a marathon, it's evident that something has happened to them, something more than just the exertion of a physical challenge.

Talking with marathoners at the completion of the Portland Marathon in 1978, Jane Underhill received this reply to her question about why one runs a marathon. "I really felt bad. My legs were gone. My arms were sore from holding them up for hours. My feet are all blistered and I've got a black toenail, and now my shoes are worn out."[4]

But this runner never considered quitting the race at any point! No, this runner faced his precipice and even took the frightening glance over the edge into a sprawling, endless abyss, but he didn't fall over that edge. That made the difference. He had passed his own version of ordeal by test; he had won a victory, and it didn't matter who finished the race ahead of him.

You can wonder at this point if the lure of distance running goes beyond masochism to the point of actual addiction. You can also ponder the consequences — *or* you can run and discover your own answers.

There are many approaches to the concept of mid-life crisis. It is the recognition of mortality and the subsequent evaluation of values; many times a radical change in behavior is a concomitant. However, one point is fairly common throughout the literature describing this phenomenon: some men suffering a midlife crisis use athletics as a way to recapture the youth that seems so important at the moment. And, although not everyone is susceptible to the dream that jogging can defy mortality, or that the "right" running shorts, the "best" shoes, or the "proper amount of cardiovascular exercise" can confer power,[5] many men specifically choose running in an effort to regain or preserve the physical and psychological well-being they fear that age is eroding.

Not everyone believes that running cures mental depression, sexual dysfunction, or heart problems, but enough people (men of all ages and women too) hope that this is true that our streets are crowded with runners.

Nor can anyone deny that there is a move on to capitalize on such fears and emphasize that people who run are the beautiful people, both inside and out, and that they run in a beautiful world. The handsome, virile male with a gorgeous, well-proportioned female at his side runs in a peaceful, green landscape unmolested by car, dog or inconsiderate nonrunners.[6]

Another pitch appeals to the jogger as masochist, as in some advertising for certain running equipment, or in a photo caption of a runner who "battles pain and distance in conquering" such-and-such race.[7] Motivations for running are numerous, but usually come back to the idea of *conquering* something — distance, time, age, and, maybe, death itself. A major factor in this need to conquer is the desire for the body to reflect the hoped-for benefits derived from running, and especially to reflect them in increased attractiveness — a supposed manifestation of one's conquest of his aging flesh.

Many men (the weaker sex when it comes to physical deterioration as a group) enter the dizzying world of running with an excess of zeal. They remember their high school days when a couple of miles was a snap; in fact, they can conjure up the days when running was as easy as staying up all night (both accomplishments a sign of immortality). Suddenly, at age thirty or thirty-five, terribly out of shape, dangerously overweight, carelessly unchecked by a physician, certain of these midlife crisis candidates discover the cure-all of distance running. Running will reduce that bulging stomach. Running will bring back the ruddy glow of healthy skin. Running will tighten the legs and rearrange some of the hourglass figure that has all of its time in the lower half. And running will turn midlife into a hunt for youth rather than a steady pilgrimage toward old age and decrepitude.

What can happen to such a middle-aged physical rebirth? Plenty. A runner not prepared for the dangers, hazards and setbacks that accompany a reunion with the physical life can become a statistic — an obituary. Running deaths continue to increase, regardless of whether or not the running subculture wishes to recognize the number.

Running subculture? What is it and who are they? How do they influence the new runner? What's their power? The running community is enormously cohesive. You can visit a week-end race anywhere in this country (and probably the world) and it is evident at once that a type of communal atmosphere exists. It may even be an atmosphere that is impossible to find in any other recreational sport (tennis, for example).

The Germans have a term for such an experience: *gemeinschaft,* a community based upon personal and intimate sharing — against that of *gesellschaft,* a community based upon a more mechanistic or impersonal sharing. The *gemeinschaft* of running is fascinating to behold. It's a community based upon mutual achievement and mutual suffering; two mutualities that lead inexorably to a bond that brings runners of all abilities and temperaments together in a spirit of understanding. It would be impossible to watch professional football players cavorting with sandlot football players; no one would expect NBA allstars to compete with weekend basketballers in a spirit of friendship and understanding.

Running has its own peculiar code of behavior geared to the subculture's propensity to reach out and make every runner a part of the event, regardless of whether that runner is world class or just able to jog above a fast walk. A marathoner is a marathoner, even if it takes him double the time to run the distance when compared to an Olympic hopeful.

The key to this *gemeinschaft* is literature. Writers and runners seem to go together. It has often been said that what places chess so far above any other game is the ability to code in shorthand the moves required to make up a contest. Everything can be read and followed because of the shorthand. Chess, therefore, has a rich history due to chessmasters who recorded their games for posterity. No one can appreciate this factor until playing out a chess game, move by move, that's over 100 years old! Even if the chessmaster has been dead for years, the games continue to teach and inspire through the remarkable pages of chess literature.

Running is somewhat like this. It isn't that dead runners inspire new runners (although that may be so to some extent), but that Frank Shorter, Bill Rodgers, George Sheehan, Joan Ullyot, and many more communicate their joy and satisfaction in running through their literary efforts. The running subculture, therefore, renews its interest and dedication with on-going information and perspectives about the exercise. Running becomes news. It becomes *now*.

A typical running magazine has articles on training, the meditative side of running, injuries and how they can be prevented, and maybe an article or two on diet. Above all, however, they contain success stories and biographical information geared for identification. (Hm, so that's what Frank Shorter eats for breakfast!) If you wish to unite a running community, just such reading material is necessary to keep people involved, interested,

24

and constantly measuring themselves against unmet but well-understood heroes. Best of all, these personal accounts and reflections keep them measuring themselves against themselves!

Running literature does all this. The magazines, those monthly manuals filled with basically identical information over and over, but in a slightly different form each time, fill the gaps for runners of all abilities and levels. They allow the fun-runner to measure himself against the AAU champion without having to take to the track and fight that kind of stiff competition. They provide both neophytes and seasoned veterans with vicarious participation in all major running events. A detailed report on the Boston Marathon, for example, brings that race and all its aspects right into the home of a serious runner. He can live the event, feel the excitement, and hope that someday he too will be able to struggle against Heartbreak Hill, or hear the applause of thousands of spectators as he crosses the finish line at Prudential Square in Boston.

One extremely fascinating part of running magazines is the advertising aimed at giving the reader additional power over his domain. Advertising provides more insights into the *gemeinschaft* he's being pulled into. For example, a sampling of running advertisements shows the following use of semantics:

"Designed for dedicated runners."
"Riding the crest of the wave."
"If you don't start running, you're going to die."
"I want to live longer!"
"Serious shoes for serious runners."
"Serious about running?"
"Whatever your favorite agony . . . "
"Peak performance."
"Run happier."
"Put fun in your jog."

Such advertisements focus on the emotional or psychological factors of running. Words such as "dedication" and "serious" appeal to the importance that running has in the runner's life. "Fun" and "happier" appeal to the playful side of the runner who is not yet into competitive running. Both types of runner, however, the serious competitor as well as the beginning jogger, share the immortality-wish that words such as "live," "die," and "agony" relate to. Language is the key to the running subculture and how it has turned a simple exercise into a multimillion dollar industry in a matter of a few years.[8]

The question persists: who is running and why are they into running with such a passion?[9] Some runners run because they believe that it's the best thing available in the way of strenuous exercise. Some run because they read and listen to runners extolling the virtues of working up a sweat on the streets of America. Or they run because, quite frankly, many consider that it's the only thing to do.[10] It's in, it's *now*. For some, it's almost like a religion, something that gives meaning and depth to their lives.

Most people run because they think it makes them feel better. They run to avoid diseases. They run to look better, both to themselves and to others. And they run because others around them don't.

Some people take up running because they consider themselves humanistic athletes; that is, they want to increase their human potential and get more out of life than is available through such of our society's current offerings as television, fast automobiles, and instant gratification. Some runners run because it relieves tension and lifts the mood.[11]

Respondents to a questionnaire[12] indicated that over 70 percent ran for fitness; just over 10 percent did it for weight control; another 10 percent or so continued running from when they were in high school or college. Approximately 7 percent took up jogging because they were proselytized. This seems to indicate that if one motivation stands out, it's the fitness concept, at least at the beginning of a runner's involvement.

The search for status shouldn't be overlooked either.

Running's in, and the outfit can make it even more so. In a Washington, D.C., suburb, a neighborhood of upper-income bureaucrats and professionals, a dignified, elderly couple do their supermarket shopping in matching blue and white jumpsuits and jogging shoes. Thereby they tastefully advertise their youthful vigor and awareness of what's "in."[13] It's what is affectionately known as *urban chic,* which includes daily jogs through the park without working up too much of a sweat.[14]

Through running, some people find a "high" that makes it all — the sweat, the potential injuries that can hobble a runner for months, the hazards from automobiles and muggings — worthwhile. Some say that running is a better "high" than any drug, way out in front of alcohol, and sometimes even better than the best sexual encounter.

Some runners run for the sheer feeling of testing the psyche against the body. *Pain* is the watchword. A runner was asked if he was ever afraid that he'd die while exerting himself in a grueling race. "Yes, I've thought of that. Maybe some day I'll collapse. My feeling is: what a lovely way to die."[15]

There are so few things in life that can be overcome by brute force and we spend a lifetime compromising with the world. So, by pushing the body to new limits that may be very slight to someone else but are limits nonetheless, we establish mastery over ourselves and in a

28

small way establish a victory over our very existence. It's what can be tagged running for the sheer hell of attacking oneself!

Marathoners have their way of establishing control:

> Then the finish. To one, it was enough to bare his behind to all present. To another it was crossing the line with a triumphant hold onto a coveted can of beer. To a married couple, it was a hand-in-hand finish. To many, it was worth sprinting the last fifty yards to beat somebody else out. And to still another, it was literally a crawl over the line, followed by a complete collapse.[16]

And some runners are into their sport because it's just that, a sport. Bill Gilbert, coach of a Pennsylvania girls' track team, calls the "manifestation of man's seemingly innate urge to play" true sport. It's "essentially a private matter like eating or making love."[17]

Whatever the motive, runners take to the roads, streets, trails and tracks in increasing numbers,[18] some driven and others driving themselves to new heights of fitness, conditioning and, oh yes, problems. It's the last of these we'll look at closely.

NOTES FROM CHAPTER ONE

1. The twenty-four-hour relay works this way: a team consists of ten runners, each running a mile in sequence. When the tenth runner

finishes his mile, he passes the baton to the first runner and the sequence starts again. No runner can be replaced once the race starts at high noon. If anyone drops out the remaining runners must close ranks and continue. The idea is to cover as many miles as possible in the twenty-four hours. This race is a test of courage as well as endurance. The intermittent rest periods are just long enough to cause cramping in the cool morning hours, but not long enough to rest for the grind ahead. One team ran 233 miles, 1160 yards in twenty-four hours.

2. Frances Knowles, "What Drives The Average Runner?" *Runner's World*, February 1976, p. 74.

3. Chic Perkins, "The Ultimate Test," *Los Angeles Herald Examiner*, 14 June 1977.

4. Jane Underhill, "Why Run the Marathon? Because It's There," *Northwest Magazine, Portland Oregonian*, 8 January 1978, p. 20.

5. Debra Woolston, "Proceed With Caution," *The Valley Times*, 8 August 1978.

6. Ibid.

7. Ibid.

8. An interesting sidelight is Jane E. Brody's article in the November 10, 1976, *New York Times* titled: "Jogging Is Like A Drug: Watch The Dosage, Beware The Problems."

9. "And pounding the pavement devoutly, fearful of disintegration if a single day is missed, makes you the sucker in the shell game, not the purveyor," as Melvin Durslag wrote in the October 30, 1978, *Los Angeles Herald Examiner*. Part of the backlash against dedicated joggers comes from the passionate feelings runners have for their chosen exercise. Many runners sneer at nonrunners, prompting Mr. Durslag to comment: "They [runners] are congesting our footpaths, invading our parks and creating eye pollution."

10. A February 19, 1977, letter to the author from the National Jogging Association ended with: "Remember, please, our cause is still on the side of the angels."

11. Researchers including Dr. John Griest at the University of Wisconsin conducted tests on two groups of depressed people. One group jogged, the other group took part in no exercise. The joggers did better overall in lifting their spirits. The *Star*, December 21, 1976.

12. A questionnaire was sent in 1977 to 100 male members of the Oregon Road Runners Club. The response by these men who were thirty-five years of age or older was a very high 80 percent. It's evident that runners enjoy talking about themselves!

13. *U.S. News and World Report,* 14 February 1977, p. 40.

14. Ibid.

15. George Leonard, *The Ultimate Athlete* (New York: Avon Books, 1977), p. 196.

16. Perkins, *The Ultimate Test.*

17. *Runner's World* editors, *The Complete Runner* (New York: Avon Books, 1974), p. 100.

18. Various reports from newspapers, radio and television claim that approximately half of America over the age of twenty exercises on a regular basis. Running, however, accounts for 5 percent to 15 percent, depending on the report and the reporter. It's almost impossible to determine the exact figure. Jim Fixx, author of the very successful *The Complete Book of Running,* feels that from 2 percent to 3 percent of the runners drop out along the way. (*Los Angeles Herald Examiner,* 5 November 1978.)

CHAPTER TWO: RUNNING:
ART, SCIENCE OR MADNESS?

"Jogging is a form of exercise in which
man transforms himself into a machine.
Chug-chug-chugging along, looking
neither to the right nor left, panting,
the 'man machine' chugs along."
Meyer Friedman and Ray H. Rosenman
Type A Behavior And Your Heart

Running has come a long way since Dr. Kenneth Cooper
first introduced his physical fitness program to this country
through the seminal book, *Aerobics,* back in 1968. Jogging
has been around a long time; it was present in this country
before Dr. Cooper reminded everyone of cardiovascular
fitness.

This kind of fitness is a state of the body whereby

a person exercising strenuously for a long time will feel little fatigue and can respond to the extreme physical demands with only a slight rise in bood pressure and pulse. This translates into endurance, stamina, and fast recovery when the exercise is over, in other words, cardiovascular fitness.

But first consider jogging in its infancy before Cooper's pet theory began to turn men and women into the streets. In those days it was a novel experience to don sweat clothes (drab grey without fancy zippers; this was the era before designer running togs and sky high prices), and move off down the street to run around the neighborhood. If you were questioned at all, (as most eccentrics are better left alone) it was to find out what you were "in training" for at the moment. Nobody was simply running for the hell of it, or for the sheer enjoyment of getting up a good sweat, or for their health.

Generally it's safe to say that running B.C. (before Cooper) was the domain of athletes preparing for the *rigors de sport.* Boxers had roadwork, football players ran laps to get their brawn into condition for the razzle-dazzle of a Saturday afternoon game, and baseball players sprinted to the outfield and back to please the manager. Very few "ordinary" folk ran just for the exercise, let alone for some vague concept such as increasing cardiopulmonary efficiency. Even spiritual regeneration[1] was not a part of running in those days. Running was for the carefully prepared athlete and not for the man or woman trying to skim down a few sizes.

Then, in the early 1970s, running came into its own and has been exploding ever since. Is it a fad? Maybe. When you consider that the popularity of jogging continues to grow at a rapid pace with each succeeding year, swelling week-end races to the point where race organizers can't cope with the crush, it looks to be faddish, yet moving toward something else.

Is it a cult? A system of community worship? Well, that's almost where running is today, but that still fails to capture the overall magnitude of what's happening to exercise in these United States.

We can close in on the magic of running by describing the phenomenon as a numenosium — a dynamic or creative force that guides people in all of their relations with society. That is a pretty big package to wrap running in; however, witness the almost religious fervor that passes through a race where thousands show up for a few hours of hell!

Running as a numen can be challenged by two types of runners. The first is the runner who has found a huge commercial profit from all of the paraphernalia that can be marketed. This runner may be of world class and ready for a business career after years of struggling through competition as an amateur. Franchising of specialty stores carrying expensive lines of running gear is one of the major fallouts from the running numenosium.

The other type of runner is the beginner or easily discouraged runner who never makes it far enough or long enough to become an addict. This kind of runner views running strictly as another panacea, another half-hearted effort at losing weight or firming muscles that have become flabby. This runner never reaches the heart of running and its mesmerizing effects.

What's in between these two types of runners? Thousands and thousands of runners quietly pursuing goals outlined for them by the running subculture, a highly literate and ambitious subculture, extremely articulate, and ever promising more than they can deliver.[2]

And this is where myths come in. A myth, according to people interested in these things, is sometimes a notion based more on tradition or convenience than fact. The world has lived with mythology since the inception of storytelling. Running too has its myths. The art of running is pronounced, announced, postulated and extrapolated from ideas promulgated by running gurus throughout the pages of more than fifty prominent books (most written in the last five years), and magazines, flashy, poshly produced, and tightly edited for maximum exposure to the numen.

Let's explore these myths and how they affect running.

More than that, let's demythologize running itself.

MYTH NO. 1: THE SMALL IS BEAUTIFUL TRAP: JOGGING IS AN INEXPENSIVE RECREATION

There's no doubt that if you talk to an experienced runner, one of the first myths he'll state as fact is that jogging is an inexpensive way to obtain the benefits of regular exercise. This is very appealing when you think of the costs involved in tennis or the new rage, racketball. However, all is not as it seems. The fact is that running shoes, the most important equipment and the mainstay of any jogger, can cost anywhere from twenty to fifty dollars a pair. Moreover, if you add replacement costs, it'll mean another ten dollars or more for manufacturer's retreads.

Sometimes it doesn't really pay to fix the shoe. Any experienced runner will tell you that shoes wear out fast. The number of miles you can get from your shoes depends on your running style, the type of surface you run on, and the product itself. Running style is the biggest problem. If you land on the far outside of the heel, the shoe can wear in a few weeks. If you add a very hard surface such as the highway, the wear is understandably increased. Finally, some brands of shoes, much like automobile tires, just wear longer than others. Any way you slice it, shoes are a big expense.

Running clothes, sweat clothes and sundry artifacts, depending on the rage of your running fever, can raise the bill considerably. There are also pedometers to help determine distance, chronographs (expensive stopwatches for the P.R.[3] fan, pacing equipment (electronic beepers to help a runner learn how to pace a distance), and a whole assortment of gadgets, aids and luxuries to turn a runner into one hell of a consumer. Perhaps the most extreme bit of equipment is the "jogging stick, an engraved, silver-tipped, 14-inch-long chunk of walnut described as the 'ultimate measure of defense against canine and car.' The cost: $20."[4]

If you add at least two pairs of shoes per year as a *minimum* requirement, running clothes, travel bag and accessories, a few of the myriad gadgets, a smattering of running books, plus a subscription or two to the top running magazines, the cost can easily come to $500 per year. It is doubtful that you can call this much outlay for a basically solo sport inexpensive!

MYTH NO. 2: THE EXTREMES FALLACY:
JOGGING IS THE ULTIMATE FITNESS EXERCISE;
IT CAN AND WILL EXTEND YOUR LIFE.

This myth falls hard, as runners who advance beyond a pedestrian mile-per-day ritual (known in some jogging circles as the boring mile syndrome) usually begin promoting the absolute qualities of running. Runners, once they progress in their exercise routine, sell running all the time, and to anyone who will listen. When it comes to extolling the alleged virtues of fitness, runners are the most optimistic people around, even when nursing injuries that keep them from pursuing their goals. Why? Easy. Everyone connected with running explains the key: run and you'll probably live forever. Oh, it's not as blunt as that, but then again, it's not too far off the mark. The words may be euphemistic, couched in fail-safe language, but the central theme remains the same.

Dr. Ernst van Aaken, coach of numerous world record holders in track and cross-country, wrote a medical treatise entitled: "Statistical Proof of a Possible Prevention of Cancer Through Years-Long Increased Endurance Functioning of Biological Oxidation, With a View of the Final Cause of Cancer."[5] Stripped down into layman's words, Dr. van Aaken was seriously suggesting that running may actually prevent certain types of cancers![6] He wrote that endurance training brings increased oxygen supply to the body's millions of cells. This in turn alleviates the malignancies that may be created by cells strangled for oxygen.[7]

If that's not enough encouragement to get you off your couch, out the front door and quickly into the street, steady running may even be the heartsaver everyone's looking for these days. In a National Jogging Association publication in 1976, it was pointed out that cardiopulmonary training will help reduce heart disease, *no matter what a fringe percentage of sedentary doctors tells us.*[8] (Emphasis mine.)

Dr. Thomas J. Bassler, a California cardiologist, tells us that anyone building stamina over a period of time to the point where a marathon can be run will never die of a heart attack. *Absolutely never.*

Is all this true? Are the facts incontrovertible and the analysis complete? Is running the one activity that provides immunity from two of mankind's greatest and most tragic killers — cancer and heart attack? Did Ponce de Leon miss the fabled fountain of youth because he arrived by horseback instead of running shoes? Is Shangrila really a running camp high in the mountains of Colorado?

Exercise, I'm sorry to say, can only do so much. It's only logical. Atrophy or lack of exercise can and will contribute to heart disease. But so can heredity. So can smoking. Your diet also plays a large part in the problem. A hyperactive nervous system reacting to the stresses and strains of modern living can virtually wipe you out before your fortieth birthday.

Runners like to point out with unabashed delight that an all-time distance champion named Clarence DeMar was found to have highly developed arteries and a heart of efficient proportions. A post-mortem on this ancient marathoner of Boston fame (who incidentally died of cancer), the man who ran in over a thousand marathons, indicated that he was indeed something special when it came to the cardiovascular system. Runners maintain that DeMar (who won the Boston Marathon seven times) developed his great circulatory system by running all those miles. He was a running machine dedicated to distance, distance and more distance.

How is that claim to be dismissed? It can't be simply turned away. However, there's a paradox here that weakens the hold runners have on their theory. Is the DeMar story the chicken or the egg? Did Clarence DeMar strengthen all those wonderful arteries to feed that mammoth heart by running all those miles, or did he bring that marvelous running machine to marathons because he was uniquely constructed to succeed at a difficult chore? After all, nothing encourages an athlete more than having the natural tools to be a winner. Clarence DeMar's arteries don't provide the answer.

Let us face the question straight on: is running really good for you at all? Yes — running is one form of exercise and exercise is marvelous for the body. The problem arises in specifying any one type of exercise, such as running, as a curative for all health problems. The body is constantly subjected to organ-wrenching stresses from internal as well as external forces. Therefore, simply eating the right foods will never assure immortality. Giving up all vices will not deliver incorruptibility. Toning down the nervous system and learning how to relax won't guarantee perennial youth. And adding a running program to any or all of these positive programs will only confuse the issue. How is one to know if running plus diet is the key or if the combination of relaxation and running is the magic one? Without an accurate yardstick on heredity, that frustrating legacy all of us receive at birth, a kind of individual clock set to self-destruct on a day hidden away in each cell, we'll never know why someone can keel over at forty after a lifetime of moderation while another person with a history of abuses continues kicking until ninety or longer.[9]

Although running — or any type of exercise — performed in moderation with your doctor's consent, will probably make you feel better, there is *no empirical evidence* that running will increase your life expectancy even one year. Most of what passes for evidence is soft data, appearances, speculation, coincidence, or wishful thinking.

MYTH NO. 3: THE NEVER LOOK BACK ARGUMENT: DANGERS FROM JOGGING ARE MINIMAL AND THOSE DANGERS THAT DO EXIST ARE FAR OUTWEIGHED BY THE BENEFITS.

This running myth probably falls hardest and is one that is vigorously defended by runners no matter what the cumulative evidence. What are the dangers? Let's begin with injuries. (We'll go into detail later on in the book.)

Automobile and overuse injuries are at the top of the list, followed by weather (including pollution), and miscellaneous accidents, such as tripping over a sprinkler, or being bitten by a dog who has read about territorial imperative and decides to exercise his rights. There's also the growing problem of muggers, especially since jogging has become more popular with women. At the risk of sounding sexist (and setting one more "group" against me), women joggers make an inviting target in a park or woodlike setting, particularly at night.

The major hazard, of course, and one that will be treated in more depth as we go on, is that of sudden exercise death (SED). This can happen to experienced runners as well as neophytes. Some little-exposed statistics are beginning to arise from the running subculture that indicate that sudden exercise death among joggers is not as isolated, and certainly not as explicable, as it once was. Every form of activity can be looked at for cost and benefits, and nothing is 100 percent good or 100 percent bad. However, running, as treated by runners, seems to be one of those endeavors that generates such enthusiasm that it is difficult to dwell on the negative aspects. But they do exist and they must be dealt with so that you can judge whether or not running is the most beneficial form of exercise for you to pursue.

MYTH NO. 4: THE JUMP ON THE BANDWAGON CONCEPT: JOGGING IS FOR EVERYBODY.

It is calculated that somewhere between six and twenty-five million Americans are running. The exact number is not known, nor how many jog on a regular basis. Running shoe manufacturers probably have the most accurate estimates, however, because their marketing program depends on solid projections to keep up steam.[10]

Science Digest estimates that Americans run about 17 billion miles per year. This comes to about 80 miles per year for every man, woman and child. Moreover, with approximately 100 calories burned for each mile covered, a 17-trillion burn total, around 500 million pounds are theoretically being shed each year. This comes to about 2.3 pounds per person!

What does this mean? Probably very little if you're not interested in the trivial points associated with a nationwide involvement with jogging. Everyone is *not* running, even if it seems that way. According to the National Jogging Association, only one-third of the people actually jogging fulfill the definition of fitness offered by the running subculture — thirty minutes of strenuous exercise at least four days per week. This means that jogging on a regular basis creates the fitness everyone's looking for these days. And to be declared fit you have to exercise at least two hours per week. This leaves us with about 2 million fit runners, no more. Not a particularly overwhelming figure!

What are the other 8 to 10 million self-proclaimed runners really doing? Some are running, but on a very inconsistent basis; some are in and out of running as the mood may strike. Both types are in danger from injuries that stem from inadequate preparation and week-ending only. In fact, an exercise-elevated pulse can turn into a killer if the owner of that pulse is not conditioned for the sudden and sustained higher-than-normal heart rate.

It is impossible to ascertain exactly how many runners are injured after attacking a running program ambitious in nature but absolutely ill conceived in execution. It is estimated that seven to ten million new joggers take to the streets, tracks, and paths of this country each year. How many remain a year later? How many have dropped out because of injuries that could have been prevented by the exercise of a little caution and an objective look at the whole jogging picture?

MYTH NO. 5: LOOKING FOR MR. CANDYBAR: JOGGING CONTROLS WEIGHT.

This myth is tough to dismiss if you stand around the starting line of any marathon race. Most of the "regulars" are not only controlling their weight, but have the emaciated look of people who have suffered through periods in a concentration camp. Runners are a skinny lot. They can be anywhere from 10 percent to 30 percent below normal weight. If you measure that against "average" weight (the weight that most of us attain in our thirties, the weight that's more than desired), it's easy to understand why runners at the starting line look thin. Body fat drops quite a bit for these competitive runners too, and it's not just cosmetic, either.

The key here is training, consistency the touchstone. No amount of exercise will burn the fat off unless it is regular, constant in intensity, and in harmony with good eating habits (poor habits being defined as too much of everything, too often). Many times an on-again-off-again jogger finds his weight declining, but after time passes the weight loss is found to be temporary. There are times when this transitory weight loss is enough of an encouragement to continue running, but when the weight again begins to show, discouragement can set in and curtail the running program.

Everything comes to those who work for it, including weight loss. The point is that it takes more than thirty minutes a day, four times a week, to make a real dent in something as difficult as losing weight. Again, running is not the cure-all, but only one part of a weight control program.

MYTH NO. 6: THE UBIQUITOUS MOVEMENT: JOGGING CREATES THE BEAUTIFUL PEOPLE.

This myth is perpetrated and perpetuated by the media. One running magazine seems to delight in showing extremely attractive men and women running through New York's Central Park, dressed in the latest jogging fashions (and without sweat to detract from the glamour!). Another running magazine featured a pretty woman on the cover, complete with tank top sans bra — a real change from the usual pictures of sweaty marathoners trying to hurdle Heartbreak Hill in the Boston Marathon!

One of the more obvious ways to beautify joggers striving to live out this myth is to add style to clothes that used to be practical but drab. It would be great if up-to-the-minute running outfits could impart to us all the benefits of running. They can't. And it would be nice if all of us could be as young, lithe, and well proportioned as the joggers featured in the running magazines. But we're not. Look around at the runners in your neighborhood. Do they look like Robert Redford and Raquel Welch? Of course not. Runners come in all shapes, sizes and outfits. Jogging remains an exercise, not a fashion show or beauty contest.

MYTH NO. 7: THE ALWAYS LOOK AHEAD SYNDROME: RUNNING'S WAY OUT IN FRONT OF ANY OTHER EXERCISE.

You may not have actually heard this myth put quite this

47

way. When runners get together, it doesn't take long before they're bragging about the way running beats all other exercises. Why? Usually it's a confusion over specificity.

Specificity is the idea that certain forms of exercise benefit certain organs and muscles. It's not reciprocal; that is, you can't train with weights and expect to hit the basketball court ready for one-on-one with a practiced basketball player. Sprinting down the local track will not build endurance. Swimming barely affects strength. Weight training is not cardiovascular because it *constricts* blood flow rather than promotes it. Karate is great for getting rid of tensions and hostilities. It may even tighten up certain parts of the anatomy. However, a karate champion would probably collapse trying to run a marathon for the first time. And calisthenics? Well, they'll make you flexible, all right, but not much else. There's no all-purpose exercise that does everything for everyone!

Think about it this way: if you eat spaghetti you ingest carbohydrates. If you're a meat person you get animal protein. You can't stuff yourself full of nothing but pasta and hope that somehow complete protein will be derived from the process of digestion. If you are what you eat, then you are what you exercise! And balance is important in both areas.

Let's explore what running can do for you *as outlined by the running subculture* in their books and magazines.

48

Jogging will improve circulation, affect pulmonary efficiency, and build strong legs. In contradistinction however, jogging will not build upper body strength and can actually accelerate stiffness, creating problems with joints and muscles that aren't used during the running period. It can also exacerbate some types of problems, like slipped discs, wrenched muscles, or dislocated joints, and bring on the "biggie" that sets most runners off the course: sudden heart attack.

Another reason why the myth exists that running is ahead of any other exercise is that the subculture constantly harps on the benefits to be derived from the exercise based on *regularity*. This reminder is shrill, strident and incessant, filling all of the literature from front to back. Runners are reminded all the time that they are engaged in the *best* form of exercise possible. In fact, no other sport, if running for exercise and fitness is a sport, claims to be so multifaceted.

An advertisement for the magazine *The Runner* exemplifies this:

> It's running as a way to health. Running as the ultimate lifesaver. Running as competition. Running as play. Running as escape. Running as philosophy. Running as a spiritual trip. Running as a way of life.[11]

This list leaves very little out — running is holistic, complete, all-encompassing. It would seem there's not much that running can't provide once you accept the idea that it's the only exercise worth exploring. Jack Batten in *The Complete Jogger* announced the benefits that come from running:

> Will jogging sharpen your thinking? Speed up your brain processes? Ease depression? Cure anxiety? Improve sleep? The answer in every case appears to be a loud yes.[12]

My survey of 100 runners in the Oregon Road Runners Club also turned up this kind of holistic response to the idea of running. The esteem running is held in is far above that of other types of recreation or exercise. Over 70 percent of the runners returning the questionnaire stated that they jog for fitness. Contrast this figure with 71 percent of the respondents who claim they've suffered injuries from that same exercise — running. What a duality!

Runners have to believe in the sanctity of their outings or discouragement would be higher than it is already. When the number of runners who have been injured in trying to be fit is on a par with the number who run for fitness, then the myth that running is so far ahead of other forms of strenuous exercise, indeed that it's the *only* strenuous exercise (no matter what the cost physically), is being subscribed to.

MYTH NO. 8: IF A LITTLE'S GOOD, MORE MUST BE BETTER: COMPETITIVE RUNNING CAN'T HURT YOU IF YOU STEP UP TO IT GRADUALLY.

Doctors should support this myth. It can keep them busy treating running injuries. Nearly half of the respondents to my questionnaire felt that the dangers inherent in running stem from two factors: training too hard, and running too far, too soon.

Look at these factors closely. The idea of training to the point of injury is the heart of what I consider the problem with running. It's overuse of the body. Overuse comes from placing a strain on joints, tendons, and muscles that eventually creates failure along the route. Stress fractures, for example, are a result of overuse and can set a runner back for months, sometimes ending all running forever. Tendonitis, another common injury, can be complicated by too much mileage without stretching exercises to compensate for the overdevelopment of certain muscles and tendons. The list of potential injuries is not endless, but wide enough so that a runner making a move from fitness to competition must be aware of it.

Competition increases the odds of a serious and debilitating injury. More runners are injured each year by stepping up to a training schedule geared for marathoning than by anything else. Many people who are running at this very moment will be out of action next year at this time. By attacking the running program the way other sports are attacked, runners can find themselves perilously close to injury. Running is a *creative exercise,* not a *skill sport.* Running should be a gentle nudge-nudge, not a heroic surge. When runners began looking at stopwatches, they should have reviewed their health insurance coverage at the same time.

When runners begin moving away from slow distance to fast competitive racing, they edge into that space where pain, injury and even sudden death are all possible. The problems associated with competition are really three-fold: (1) Too much mileage brings out weaknesses in the individual body; (2) Too much speed brings on the possibility of a collapse point; (3) Running against others can mean running at someone else's level of strength, not your own.

The difference between fitness running and competitive running is the difference between jogging for health and jogging for a place. The former can be pleasurable, health-inducing and a tonic; the latter can produce severe complications. The choice is with every runner (with a little help from the running subculture).

MYTH NO. 9: THE DO AS I SAY FORMULA: IF A RUNNING DOCTOR SAYS SO, IT MUST BE TRUE

The running subculture is blessed with gurus, many of

them physicians. Some of these sages, in fact, have been given demigod status. Dr. George Sheehan of New Jersey, for example, a cardiologist and runner, is in demand as a speaker all across the country. His books are filled with philosophy as well as practical advice for the runner. In his books, Dr. Sheehan quotes liberally from philosopher and runner alike. Dr. Kenneth Cooper is so well known and respected that some countries call cardiovascular exercise "taking the Cooper."

These "running doctors" help the sport even in the face of adversity. A champion runner is looked up to because he scaled the mountains we all stand and admire but lack the talent or courage to climb. But even more impressive is a medical practitioner telling us about the positive attributes of running and then going out and practicing what he preaches. That's inspiring.

So how can it be wrong? Easy. There is no consensus in the medical community as to the benefits from running. There is especially no consensus when it comes to the dangers of running. There are doctors who are against running as well as doctors who are all for it. There are probably as many doctors who think swimming is just as marvelous for increasing fitness but who aren't as caught up in promoting their form of exercise. Running, unlike most other forms of exercise, seems to have an abundance of literary talent to insure that running doctors have their forum. Those who oppose running aren't going out of their way to publish beautiful magazines or open sporting goods stores with wall-to-wall running equipment. How many books even mention the doctors who condemn the widespread abuse of cardiovascular exercise?

MYTH NO. 10: THE SOUR GRAPES SYNDROME: ANYONE WHO KNOCKS RUNNING IS EITHER NOT INTERESTED IN EXERCISE, OR FOR SOME REASON HAS GIVEN UP RUNNING.

Runners have to keep their morale up if they're to continue to exercise with intensity. Competitive runners don't need anything to keep them going because they have next week-end's ten-miler, or April's contribution to collective masochism, the Boston Marathon. By and large, however, the rest of the joggers putting in their weekly mileage to stay on top of their fitness program need to believe that what they're doing is absolutely correct and without detractors. It's hard to keep going with nagging doubts.

The negative side of anything is unappealing, especially if that something eats up a major portion of your time and energy. When you think of the numerous books already written about running, you'll see that knocking running is about as popular as selling buggy whip franchises at an automobile convention. It just isn't done.

Why? Many reasons. Some are as natural as the human condition itself. Some, on the other hand, are for personal reasons, such as financial gain (and can be looked at with a jaundiced eye). Runners are like everyone else, only more so. They want to be a special breed set apart from the rest of humanity. Who doesn't? They want to have something that's unique, an endeavor that separates the mighty from the miniscule, something that can be shared with others who have the same predilection. They want to create a language, a subculture and a community based upon running as a tonic, running as an exercise. Running, as the magazine put it, as life! You find this kind of cohesiveness in chess, bridge, tennis, and countless other "games" where *belonging* is almost as important as doing.

NOTES FROM CHAPTER TWO

1. See Joe Henning's *Holistic Running: Beyond the Threshold of Fitness* (New York: New American Library, 1978), and Mike Spino's *Beyond Jogging: The Innerspaces of Running* (Millbrae, California: Celestial Arts, 1976), for running as a mystical experience (or a quasi-religious undertaking).

2. An interesting article on promising more than can be delivered is "Running is Debated as Benefit to Heart," Bayard Webster, *New York Times,* 28 October 1976.

3. Personal record. Most runners are caught up in how fast they can cover a piece of ground. Since most of us can never legitimately tackle a record, we have to be satisfied by going after our own records. This means continually running faster to obtain a P.R.

4. Portland *Oregonian,* 21 October 1978.

5. Ernst van Aaken, *The van Aaken Method: Finding the Endurance to Run Faster and Live Healthier* (Mountain View, California: World Publications, 1976), p. 34.

6. My survey (see appendix) indicated that over 4 percent of the respondents thought that running prevented cancer. These same people checked off almost every item provided on the questionnaire, leading me to believe that there is a significant number of runners who feel running is a curative and can lead to immortality.

7. van Aaken, *van Aaken Method,* p. 37.

8. Rory Donaldson, "Ken Cooper and The Aerobics Center," *National Jogging Association Review,* 1976, p. 6.

9. For an interesting excursion into the common denominators for longevity, a delightful little book is George Gallup's *The Secret of Long Life* (New York: The Curtis Publishing Company, 1959). Gallup, with the help of Evan Hill, sampled a cross-section of the 29,000 Americans older than ninety-five in 1950. The consensus seemed to be that many diverse factors go into longevity; e.g., eating habits, exercise programs, the handling of stress, etc. However, one of the most important seemed to be heredity; how long did your parents live? It seems that the cliche that states "pick your parents carefully" holds true.

Interesting reading along this line is William B. McCafferty's article "Does A Threshold Age Cancel Longevity Hopes of Exercisers?" *The Physician and Sports Medicine,* June 1975.

10. Blue Ribbon Sports, manufacturers of the Nike running shoes, second only to Adidas of West Germany, began in 1963 in a Portland, Oregon, basement. In 1972 sales were $3,900; 1977 sales topped $2.5 million dollars. Nike cracked the price barrier in 1979 with the first running shoe over $50. *Willamette Week,* 30 October 1978.

11. Advertisement from *The Runner,* New Times Publishing Company, 1978.

12. Jack Batten, *The Complete Jogger* (New York: Harcourt Brace Jovanovich, Inc., 1977), p. 78.

CHAPTER THREE: CARS, DOGS, MUGGERS AND OTHER DRAGONS IN THE STREET

> "Cars will swerve the moment drivers
> spot you, and how early they swerve
> indicates how clearly you are being
> seen. If they don't swerve until they're
> five yards away, you need a different
> wardrobe — and paid-up insurance."
>
> James F. Fixx
> *The Complete Book of Running*

Running has many types of hazards. Physical dangers will be covered in the next chapter, but here we'll examine those injuries and fatalities resulting from external factors; for example, automobiles, muggers and other nasty things that can face a runner out for a jaunt. We'll break these external problems down into two categories: (1) those caused by the runner himself; and (2) those caused by the world at large.

External problems caused by the runner himself include the ever-present danger from moving vehicles driven by people unprepared or, worse yet, unwilling to share the road with joggers. This danger is present in *broad daylight* as well as at night. If you've ever run on a crowded highway filled with fast moving vehicles, you quickly learn that the difference between being struck and being missed is the difference between a fraction of a second and a missed heartbeat. It's just that close, and can leave you shaken and very uncomfortable. Sometimes, depending on how masochistic you're feeling, playing "chicken" can be exhilarating. When you're running down a busy highway with the wind softly at your back and the cars whizzing by so close that side view mirrors are within inches of your head, the feeling can be euphoric; you're challenging this mechanistic world to move over and make room for a human being. It's like Russian roulette with every chamber loaded with shells except one!

In Michigan, to illustrate, a driver was indicted for felonious assault with an automobile after he aimed his car at a runner jogging down a local street. The runner, however, happened to be an off-duty police officer and was quick enough to take down the license number.

Truman R. Clark of the *Los Angeles Times* writes that he's been running on roads and sidewalks for ten years and has run in six different states around the country. During that decade the reporter has had three automobiles deliberately aimed at him.[1]

Why are auto drivers out to "get" runners? For openers, runners and cars don't go well together on the road. The highway is really not a healthy environment for someone on foot. A runner is very hard to see. A runner is likely to be someplace where he shouldn't be in relation to the vehicle itself, such as the middle of an intersection where drivers are trying to figure out where all the other traffic is going. I've seen intersections with four-way stop signs where runners cut across the traffic lanes while drivers are intent on making it before the next vehicle. The runner is never really taken into account. Many times a rush hour traffic jam finds a runner threading his way through the cars filled with angry, frustrated and impatient drivers. It's not a good mix and it never will be, no matter how many joggers are on the streets in the future.

Sometimes a driver becomes infuriated seeing a runner ahead of him. If the runner should get in the way and accidentally slow the driver's pace, all hell can break loose. Truman Clark reports that runners training along New York's Riverside Drive, in 1977, were run down by a car driven by someone aiming at the group. The driver was allegedly having "fun." It was no joke for the men on their feet — and three of them ended up in the hospital.[2]

Can drivers of cars be jealous of runners? Yes. Sometimes a driver will become incensed when he sees the lean, trim runner moving steadily along to one side of his vehicle. The result, depending on the degree of upset at the moment, is a close call, or, if you were on Riverside Drive in 1977, a possible trip to the hospital.

There isn't a runner extant who doesn't have a story or two of near-misses on the street. Sometimes the story doesn't have a happy ending.

How many joggers are injured each year by moving vehicles? It's hard to make that estimate, but if 8,300 pedestrians were killed and 100,000 more injured on the highways and streets of America in 1977, some proportion belongs to the runner.[3] Unfortunately the danger is growing. More and more runners report problems associated with the automobile.

How bad can it really be out there on the streets of America? Here's what marathoner Bill Rodgers has to say about it: "He aimed the car at me and tried to run me down. His face was contorted with rage. He scared me half to death."[4] An Ithaca, New York, man was indicted on the charge that he repeatedly took aim at marathoners with his pickup truck. The man was acquitted by a jury. They thought the felony charge was too extreme![5]

One way for runners to avoid being run down by drivers who are not out to maim them but who just can't see them in the dark is to use special clothing or equipment. Vests are available that have a reflective material that helps the runner stand out among dark objects when illuminated by headlights. There are also shoes with reflective stripes. You can purchase reflective tape and stickers that give drivers a chance to see the slow moving object in the darkness. Any or all of these aids is probably a wise investment, considering the alternative of medical bills, pain killers and artificial limbs.

Of course, not all problems related to the auto are the driver's fault. Not by a long shot. Some runners have nasty dispositions, and when it comes to sharing the road with two-ton vehicles, they aren't very friendly. In fact, there seems to be a strong objection to moving out of the way:

> . . . the crazy truth is that many joggers, moving in breezy triumph down a highway or dark street, develop a streak of testy arrogance and refuse to budge for an oncoming or following car.[6]

Ironically, one of the most severe accidents in the running community was that suffered by Ernst van Aaken in 1971. The originator of LSD — long, slow distance running — and the coach of many champions, van Aaken was struck by a truck while running at night and lost both legs.

He's not the only one. Limbs have been lost by other runners but none so famous and with such importance to the running world as van Aaken.

And people can be killed while running. The reports don't overwhelm the running community because its members have accepted this hazard as a price to be paid for being an iconoclastic athlete. For example, one young member of the New York Road Runners Club was struck and killed one night near Kennedy Airport.[7]

When you analyze the conditions that create hazards for a runner out on the street, they can be broken down into components. One component is not using highway separations that are made for bikes and pedestrians; the runner ends up out on the road where the automobile is the absolute king. Wide shoulders on a highway are better than no shoulders at all. Bad lighting is many times superior to no lighting at all. And poor weather is better than bad weather when visibility is near zero. It is a help when the runner is running *against* the traffic so that there is less chance of something sneaking up from behind. And finally, defensive running is something that few runners think about when they're out on the highway, but they should. It can mean life — or a trip to the county morgue.[8]

Attacks on runners fall into two categories: those perpetrated by other people, and those by dogs (or other wildlife).

Being attacked by another person is nothing new. We've had muggings for as long as anyone can remember. However, with the advent of so many runners taking to the streets, parks and woods, mugging has become a special problem for the jogger. The increase in attacks is something that every runner should face, especially women. A letter to the National Jogging Association points up the urgency of this problem:

It is with great sadness and outrage that I write to you. I write especially to warn other women who might be like me — that is, love to run and love to run alone as a soul-nurturing experience. We can no longer do this and be safe.

About a month ago, as I was running in the morning along a path that I have run hundreds of times, a young man with a knife assaulted me from behind some bushes and tried to rape me. Fortunately for me, I was able to fight him off and escape with very little physical harm. However, the experience has deeply affected me, and has really shaken my cool. I am a middle-aged woman and had never thought of myself as vulnerable to such experiences. Being attacked certainly changed all that for me. Women, do not run alone. Since this experience I have found other women friends who are willing to work out schedule problems so that we can offer one another safety. What has been lost in privacy and alone time running is now made up by a sense of community and safety.[9]

Truman Clark adds that in Venice, California, a woman was cornered by two thugs in a beachfront parking lot after dark. She managed to break away and outrun the attackers, thereby "winning her first race."[10]

In early summer of 1975, a woman running alone near her home at night was brutally attacked by an unknown assailant. He used a concrete block to break every bone in her face. After a year of expensive and painful reconstructive surgery, the woman is running again.[11]

Dr. Joan Ullyot writes that three of her friends in three different cities across the country have been attacked while running. "All three of my friends," Dr. Ullyot points out, "were attacked from behind, one of them in broad daylight. Both national class marathoners, they were out on training runs in areas much used by joggers, so on hearing footsteps behind them, both women felt semi-amused at 'another fragile male ego' intent on passing a mere woman. Next thing they knew, they were grabbed by the neck. Fortunately, both of these women escaped unraped by fighting back, struggling, or screaming. The third, attacked at dusk in a deserted area, was not so lucky."[12]

But men are not immune to hostility and injury either. In Maryland, a badly assaulted runner was hospitalized for a month and nearly lost the sight of one eye. How did he receive such a beating? He had unwisely shouted at two drunken men in a pickup truck who had nearly run him down on a deserted road. The men had stopped the truck, got out, and ambushed the unsuspecting runner.[13] He was lucky. He could have been killed.

It is argued that runners are no more frequently attacked than walkers out for an evening stroll, or shoppers crossing a parking lot at some suburban mall. This may be true. However, runners make inviting targets for three main reasons. Most runners work out alone, carry no weapons (and have little opportunity to even conceal one), and often work out in private, secluded spots that place them away from traffic congestion (and out of sight of help).

It's true that working out alone has its advantages. It's the time when a runner can experience the metaphysical side of existence and just listen to the body. It's the time to commune with nature or just be with oneself. However, a lone runner is a sitting duck when it comes to attacks.

Carrying a weapon could very well be worth the effort involved. Some runners wisely take along a stick with a nail in the head. This is usually reserved for fighting off dogs, but can sometimes discourage someone out to do no good. The same goes for a mace-type spray that can be purchased at most pet wholesalers. These weapons don't make the runner impervious to attack, but they do provide an opportunity to test the courage of the mugger.

Most joggers find their perfect spot for running and then return there time after time. It can be a bucolic trail, a country road with little traffic, the meandering path through a pretty local park, or just a lonely, secluded area that provides some relief from the pressures of daily life. It also provides the perfect setting for an attacker.

Whether you're a veteran jogger or a beginning, it's a good idea to look at your running habits and determine if you're a possible target for attack. You may want to make some changes in the location or time that you run, changes that might just save your life.

If you've ever faced an angry dog, you know the terror that can be experienced. It's a situation that adds little to the pleasure of fitness. The problem comes from territorial imperative, that instinct which causes an animal to stake out a piece of ground (usually by the irritating habit of urinating all over every shrub, bush and telephone pole), and defending it against any and all intruders. A runner can cross into a dog's territory without even being aware that he has done so. Almost immediately he's faced with a growling, snarling animal who's very upset over the intrusion. Whether or not the dog is just making a fuss, putting up a front, or is actually prepared to eject the intruder depends on the circumstances, the fear generated within the runner, and the size of the dog making the fuss.

My experience has been that barking and snarling are

two different signals. A barking dog may or may not come after a jogger. A snarling dog, on the other hand, is extremely upset and can become an instant menace if not treated with the utmost caution. If a runner is really scared by a barking dog, he increases his chances of an attack. Dogs quickly sense fright and become bolder when they realize their opponent is not willing to face the contest.

The most important aspect is the dog's size. For some reason, smaller dogs — the breeds that seem to be the most nervous and can run in and out between your feet — are the ones that make straight for your ankles. Larger dogs would sooner frighten you out of their territory and remain uncontested. There are no hard and true facts to back this up, and every situation concerning a frightened or frenzied dog should be treated with care. I've known runners who were knocked flat by large dogs and some who managed to scare little canines to death by screaming at them, a type of barking and snarling back that lets the dog know who's boss!

Would you believe that dogs aren't the only natural hazards around? Richard Lees of Overland Park, Kansas, wrote to *Runner's World* that during a very pleasant Sunday morning jog he was attacked from behind and pecked on the head by a large bird. His knees gave way and he fell to the ground, bleeding. *Runner's World* reported that his experience is not unique among runners[14] and I can attest to that. I was running along one fine spring morning when I happened to pass under a large tree. I didn't see the nest in the tree, but the mother bird definitely saw me. She swooped and screamed and nearly took my head off as I passed close to her home. A couple of days later I made the same run and was nearly pecked on the head again. I very wisely changed running courses for a few months.

All external problems caused by nature stem from the extremes of weather. If it's too hot or too humid, a runner is in real danger. If it's too cold and the wind is biting, the runner can also be in jeopardy. And we must consider too man's contribution — air pollution — a danger easily dismissed by many city runners who can't avoid the stuff. Pollution can really place a runner in trouble. Let's look at these problems individually.

There are a couple of problems that can plague a runner facing heat. One is heat exhaustion and the other is heat stroke.

Heat exhaustion is a state of shock in which the runner has a weak pulse, increased sweating (while the skin remains cool and moist to the touch), and shallow breathing. Nausea, vomiting, dizziness or fainting can also occur. If this condition is not treated, *it can lead to death.*

Heat stroke is even more serious because it is more demanding of countermeasures such as bed rest, need for fluids, and total restriction of sedation. It is characterized by a slowing of the pulse, dizziness, increased body temperature, dehydration, and a very dry skin. Sweating drops off, leaving the body defenseless against its heating problem. Convulsions or unconsciousness can occur. *Heat stroke kills runners. And it kills quickly.*

How much danger is there from hyperthermia (heat stroke, heat exhaustion and muscle cramps)? The experts seem to agree on this point: plenty of danger exists, and runners have died taking part in races where heat stroke overcame them. Heat stroke and its by-product, kidney failure, are associated with marathoning in the hot sun.[15] The hazard of heat stroke lurks behind every race run in temperatures that soar above 80°F. When too much humidity is added, the combination can be lethal. High humidity and high temperatures can dehydrate a runner in a very short time. The weight loss at this point is substantial and it's not the dreaded fat that is melting away, but vital fluids. When the fluid balance becomes too far out of line, the runner faces immediate collapse and the chance of a more serious aftermath — kidney failure. If the kidneys cease functioning, you have a possible fatality.

"Violent chills, spinning head, black spots before my eyes just past the sixteen-mile mark. Had only one gulp of Gatorade, no water, and lost twelve pounds." This was written by a veteran runner who dropped out of the 1973

Boston Marathon. He was fortunate as a dozen or so runners ended up in the hospital and *one died.* Almost 400 of the runners had to be helped back to the finish line. It was 79°F. that day in Boston.[16]

Many runners ignore heat. They just don't realize the dangers involved with the sudden onset of hyperthermia. For example, my survey of the Oregon Road Runners Club produced some bizarre responses to a question on running in the heat. I asked for the warmest temperature the runner worked out in over his career. The mean, or average, was a startling 93.6°, with one respondent claiming to have run in 115° with an ice pack on his head! With an average of 93.6°, this means some runners were well above that extremely uncomfortable temperature. And since physicians have warned that *any* exercise attempted in 90° temperatures or above is dangerous, no matter how well adapted the runner *thinks* he is to the heat, the respondents were telling me the depth of their unconcern for this killer.

Yet despite the attitude of some runners toward the dangers, they can really heat up when the temperature begins to climb. It has been noted that a rectal temperature of 105°F. is possible during an extended run on a very hot day. Sweat loss may be between 6 percent and 10 percent of the runner's total weight.[17] In short, the body is placed under a tremendous strain by the heat and can collapse if pushed beyond its individual endurance level.

This goes for healthy joggers as well as those people with problems that are severely complicated by heat.

Many important races are run when the temperature is beyond the safe zone. The Boston Marathon, for example, annually draws crowds of runners that compete in all kinds of weather. Boston in late April can be cool and wet or warm and quite humid. The 1973 race, with the temperature at 79°, was one of the most dangerous in the long history of this grueling event. It was the highest on record for that area on April 16. Few runners had prepared for the kind of day it was to be on the streets of Boston and surrounding communities that make up the 26.3 mile race. Only about 600 of the 1400 starters who were capable of running three and one-half hours or better actually ran that fast. Almost a dozen runners ended up in the hospital with heat exhaustion, and hundreds of others walked into the finish many hours after the race was officially over.[18]

I watched the Culver City Marathon in the late 1950s, when heat and heavy Los Angeles air pollution combined to almost destroy a friend. The temperature was well into the lower 90s when he came around the turn on his twentieth mile, staggering like a drunk coming home from an all-night bash. He finally fell into the arms of a race official and was taken to the hospital. He nearly died from the experience. He didn't run again for two months.

The twenty-four-hour marathon relay I took part in

during July of 1977 was held during a very hot weekend in Portland, Oregon. I drank a can of Gatorade after each mile (about forty-five minutes between miles and Gatorade), to keep from dehydrating.

During the daylight hours of the relay it was over 90°. It amazed me that as the relay runners took their turns and then headed for the shade between miles, others working out on the track were circling lap after lap without any fluids for replacement. The one small fountain situated in a remote part of the field was never really used by these foolhardy joggers.

Dehydration and the approach of heat exhaustion are difficult to imagine if you haven't gone through the experience. I had been running twenty miles on National Jogging Day in 1976 when it happened — sudden dehydration. It was a warm morning and I hadn't taken any fluids for the whole time I was out on the run. I was in the first stages of collapse when the awareness of my problem came with a kind of confusion, a lack of direction, a strange feeling that I wasn't getting anywhere. And I wasn't. Another runner close behind me kept asking me if I felt all right. I found myself wanting to answer but not making any response. I was wobbling and very near to tripping over the curb. When I finished the twenty miles there were spots before my eyes and I had a light-headed feeling. I was sweating heavily but felt extremely cold to the touch.

If I had continued running it could have meant my life!

The simple but effective way to avoid problems while running in the heat is — fluids. Drink plenty of liquid — water, iced tea, Gatorade, whatever you prefer — *before* you start the race or workout. Then, while you're running, stop frequently (every fifteen minutes or so) for more liquids — not just a sip but a good drink. Don't feel that you're wasting time by doing this. You could be saving your life. And incidentally you're not harming your speed. Keeping the body fluids in balance, avoiding overheating, helps your body perform most efficiently.

Just as dangerous a problem and probably more common is that of hypothermia, the sudden onset of shock from being cold and wet. Hypothermia has been known as the killer of the unprepared. It is a devastating reaction and an experienced runner should not shrug it off.

Hypothermia means loss of body heat, or more precisely a lowering of the temperature of the body's inner core. In acute accidental hypothermia, the loss of heat from the body's vital core can result in uncontrollable shivering, followed by increasing clumsiness and loss of judgment, and a fairly rapid lapse into unconsciousness. If nothing is done to reverse the condition, *death will follow.* [19]

There are some misconceptions about hypothermia which can get a runner into trouble and jeopardize his life.

73

First, exposure doesn't mean much, taken by itself. Hypothermia is a product of exposure, but it takes a certain set of very defined conditions which are available outside your front door, as well as on a mountain peak, to destroy a runner who isn't being careful.

Second, altitude is *not the key to hypothermia*. You don't have to be on top of a mountain to suffer hypothermia. An ill-equipped and unthinking jogger can suffer at sea level, as well as an ill-equipped and unthinking climber at 20,000 feet above the ocean floor.

Third, extremely low temperatures are not required for hypothermia to appear. This is probably the most dangerous misconception a runner can have about the potential problems from cold weather. People have gone into shock and actually *died* from hypothermia when the temperature was above freezing!

What are the conditions that can kill you while running (or at least send you to the hospital for some recuperation time)? The elements needed for the problem are cold, wetness and wind and the difficulty of staying warm and dry.

When a runner is cold and wet from the rain or fog, or even his own perspiration, wind will evaporate the water from the skin quickly, taking with it heat. If the heat loss is great enough, the runner will begin to suffer from the effects of exposure. If the heat loss goes on long enough, the runner will be forced into hypothermia. Most wet clothes, especially sweat suits made from anything but a cotton material, will remain damp during a workout. This dampness can accelerate the heat loss leading to hypothermia.

The wind chill factor plays an integral part in the problem of hypothermia. Wind blowing on damp skin will drop the skin temperature many degrees below the surrounding temperature. For example, a 40 m.p.h. wind during a modestly cold 40° day will produce a wind chill factor of 10°F. on a runner's damp skin. If it is near freezing where you run, a 40 m.p.h. wind will provide a skin temperature of about minus 3°![20]

Three deaths occurred from hypothermia during the annual Four Inns Walking competition on the English moors in late March of 1964. This contest involved a forty-five-mile walk at elevations ranging from 650 to 2000 feet above sea level. Three-man teams started at two-mile intervals over the prescribed course, which was equipped with checkpoint marks of three to eight miles. At each checkpoint a first aid rescue team stood by and hot drinks were available to the contestants. The weather at the beginning was cloudy with a light drizzle. There was a wind, but it wasn't much to think about. However, later on during the event, the rain became heavier and the winds picked up with occasional strong gusts. During the night the weather became dangerous; sleet and snow pelted the walkers and the temperature dropped to 35°. The wind was reaching 38 m.p.h.

Three walkers died that night and five had narrow escapes. Only 22 out of 240 competitors finished the walk. It was a disaster.[21]

The key to hypothermia is in exercise — the very thing the runner is doing in the cold, wet and windy weather. Exercise produces body heat and the heat is carried away by the skin. What follows is a loss of core temperature and the harbinger of hypothermia. It can be prevented by wearing fabrics that breathe — that means cotton — and avoiding running on cold, wet, and windy days.

How seriously do runners take the dangers associated with the cold? My survey indicated that cold is taken less seriously than heat! Hypothermia remains that distant cousin related to the mountains and mountaineering. Runners can't conceive of the danger being around the corner or over at the local park.

Hypothermia is the extreme case developing from cold weather. There are other problems too, not as serious, but nonetheless dangerous for the runner not watching for any problems. Cold stress can afflict a runner who fails to warm up properly before running off for the daily workout. If muscles are not prepared for the cold, a biomechanical breakdown can result. The same goes for lung burn, the ingestion of frigid air. Most runners ignore this problem and have been advised by magazines and books to disregard its potential. But it *can't be ignored* if you wish to be safe. Cold air taken in through the mouth bothers some runners. I've run with people who find that cold air gives them a severe pain in the chest and brings on asthmalike symptoms. Whether or not this can lead to injury or illness is a matter of speculation.

The most severe of the minor problems from the cold is that of frostbite. Frostbite can result in permanent impairment. When tissue dies it can become gangrenous and lead to additional dangers for the runner. Frostbite is rare among runners, but it can happen!

The third danger after heat and cold is the current phenomenon of modern industrial society, air pollution. And what a problem it is! Sometimes a city runner will wonder if the positive health gain from exercise isn't being offset by running where pollution is heaviest. It is something to think about and an area that will undoubtedly be covered more closely by running magazines in the near future. The last word has not been heard.

The element that is most bothersome in air pollution from a runner's standpoint is that of carbon monoxide – a by-product of the internal combustion engine. Wherever automobiles are in large supply, carbon monoxide builds up in huge quantities. The problem with carbon monoxide

77

is that it interferes with the oxygen exchange between lungs and blood supply; the interference is like trying to breathe at high altitudes. There isn't enough oxygen to go around. This puts a strain on the cardiovascular system, since running is pushing the heart and taxing the circulatory system. If the body's demands aren't met, the result could be significant.

There are other noxious factors in pollution. For example, sulfur oxides in combination with solid particulates, or photochemical smog to the layman, can be horrendous and is well known to runners in the Los Angeles area.[22]

Rick Trujillo, a Colorado runner of fame, normally runs on mountain trails in only the cleanest of air. He writes: "One day a friend and I went on a fifteen-mile run along an easily-travelled two-way road with cars passing every five to ten seconds. One mile from the finish, he stopped. I was forced to stop later due to a sudden difficulty in breathing. The attack on our breathing came suddenly and seemingly without warning. After stopping, breathing became normal. But any attempt to run or even walk immediately brought back the panting and feeling of suffocation. It took twenty to thirty minutes for our breathing to become normal enough for us to finish the last mile. The feeling of shortness of breath lasted several hours after the run."[23]

Shortness of breath and a kind of nausea, including the

feeling of being dizzy, are all symptoms of too much pollution.

One of the less-talked-about side effects that could make running in high levels of carbon monoxide even more dangerous is that of impaired judgment. Concentrations of carbon monoxide that surpass normal levels can result in a runner suffering blurred vision, experiencing light-headedness, and running along in a stumbling manner. If the runner is particularly close to the vehicles spewing out the pollution, it could mean further trouble. It is possible that some accidents have been caused by a runner getting too close to a car while suffering from pollution intoxication.

Dr. Edward P. Flanagan, a onetime Boston Marathon runner, is quoted in the *Los Angeles Times* as saying, "Life is too short to spend your recreation swallowing other people's smoke."[24] He advises runners to choose their environment carefully.

One of the complaints heard from marathoners is that if you're up with the leaders in the race it means gagging on air pollution. Most races provide lead automobiles to keep the path open for the runners. Some marathoners have had to swallow fumes for the entire race!

NOTES FROM CHAPTER THREE

1. Truman Clark, "Thugs, Hostile Drivers Have Joggers On The Run," *Los Angeles Times,* 29 June 1978.

2. Ibid.

3. Victor F. Zonana, "Joggers And Drivers Have More Run-ins in Streets and Court," *Wall Street Journal,* 22 March 1978.

4. Ibid.

5. Ibid.

6. Batten, *Complete Jogger,* p. 59

7. George A. Sheehan, *Dr. Sheehan on Running* (Mountain View, California: World Publications, 1975), p. 40.

8. Another problem is that of lack of identification. Many joggers run without any kind of identification at all. It's not uncommon to hear of a runner out for an evening jog who is struck by an automobile and rendered unconscious. Without any way for the police to determine who the runner is, dangerous complications can arise if treatment can't be started without someone's permission.

9. *The Jogger,* 9, no. 1 (February 1977).

10. Clark, "Thugs, Hostile Drivers."

11. Kathryn Lance, *Running For Health and Beauty: A Complete Guide for Women* (Indianapolis, Indiana: Bobbs-Merrill Co., Inc., 1977), p. 98.

12. Joan Ullyot, *Women's Running* (Mountain View, California: World Publications, 1976), p. 85.

13. Clark, "Thugs, Hostile Drivers."

14. *Runner's World,* September 1978, p. 126.

15. *Runner's World, The Complete Runner,* p. 185.

16. *Runner's World* Editors, *Running With The Elements,* (Mountain View, California: World Publications, 1974), p. 13. The runner who died was forty-four-year-old Harold Gale from Connecticut.

17. Ibid., p. 24.

18. Ibid., p. 15.

19. Theodore G. Lathrop, *Hypothermia: Killer of the Unprepared* (Portland, Oregon: Mazamas, 1975), p. 1.

20. Ibid., p. 7.
21. Ibid., p. 9.
22. *Runner's World, Running With The Elements*, p. 57.
23. Ibid., p. 58.
24. "Warning to Joggers: You'll Choke on Smoke." *Los Angeles Times*, 26 August 1977. Another interesting article along the same line is Harry Daniell's "Try Not to Exhaust Yourself," *Runner's World*, September 1976.

CHAPTER FOUR: SWEATING AND COURAGE: AN UNHOLY ALLIANCE

"The majority of my athletic patients
are runners."

Steven I. Subotnick
The Running Foot Doctor

The dangers from running cannot be ignored. Injuries, once relegated to the back pages of running magazines, are now featured boldly. If you run a little, you stand a chance of being hurt; if you run a lot, it's almost a sure thing. The only unknown is the extent of your injuries.

Running and shoes are probably as synonymous as any two terms in athletics. They go together like marijuana and a good high. It's hard to think of one without thinking of the other.

Shoes are to a runner what tires are to a racing car:

performance, protection and basic to the success of the entire operation. The right tire won't guarantee a championship ride, but the wrong tire will destroy any chance of finishing a race in good position.

What is simple is the running itself. Shoes make it more complicated and more vital. We are the only animal that needs to put something over our feet before we enter the outside world. Why? *Injury.* Human feet are fragile, less than desirably flexible, and prone to injury if they are exposed too long to hard surfaces, not counting sharp rocks and some of the more vicious manmade surfaces that even shoes fail to protect from. It's settled — the human foot must be covered if we're to walk or run any distance repeatedly.

Jogging can be dangerous to the feet, but it can be absolutely devastating to the knees. Jogging downhill places a terrific strain on the knees, so much so that some people have had to give up running because of the resultant problems.[1]

While knee injuries are the number one problem and probably the most written about complaint, jogging can become lethal if such seemingly insignificant items as blisters aren't carefully attended to when first forming. There is a definite danger for distance competitors who push themselves during a long, hard race after developing severe blisters. You can't very well pause during a marathon to treat blisters! Some racers have actually completed a long distance race with a shoe filled with blood. But blisters left unattended can kill.[2]

Overall musculoskeletal problems break down into four common ailments: (1) strains; (2) sprains; (3) stress fractures; and (4) tendinitis.[3]

A strain is usually classified as a tear. The tear comes between the muscle-tendon pair and can leave scar tissue that is not as flexible as the original cellular structure.[4] The runner can overcome a strain if the healing is good and the return to running is aided by stretching exercises to prevent a relapse.

A sprain is usually a tear in the ligament.[5] These sprains are near joints and can easily place a jogger out of commission for months, if not forever. Running with an injured ligament is almost a sure-fire method for cutting a jogging career very short.

A stress fracture is basically minor bone damage.[6] When the bone closes over the small break we have a ready-to-run athlete. However, sometimes the stress fracture is difficult to diagnose and can be mistreated by the doctor in attendance. The result is another invitation to disaster.

Tendinitis is the inflammation of the tubular sheath surrounding a tendon.[7] The two most common areas of tendinitis are around the heel (Achilles tendinitis) and about the very fragile knee (chondromalacia). Together, these two areas of inflammation account for a majority of the injuries associated with running. It's hard to find a runner who hasn't at one time or another been plagued by Achilles tendinitis or chondromalacia.

What are the injury rates for runners? Are they extreme and something to be concerned about? Many figures are quoted as to injuries; many runners have been questioned and surveys taken. In a 1971 survey of its readership, *Runner's World* magazine found that the leading injury site, as expected, was the kneecap (18 per cent). The next highest category was Achilles tendinitis (14 per cent); shin splints came third (11 per cent). Arches and ankles accounted for approximately 7 per cent each, foot fracture 5 per cent, calf injuries 4 per cent, while hips, heels and hamstrings averaged about 3 per cent. The bottom of this list included thighs and leg fractures (each about 1 per cent).[8]

What creates these injuries? Why will almost one out of every five runners be stopped dead in their tracks by aching or swollen kneees? The answer, according to most running pundits, can be divided into two categories:

(1) Too much running and probably too much speed
    to go with the extra distance;
(2) Something radically wrong with the runner's
    musculoskeletal equipment.

If a jogger runs too far, too fast, wearing shoes not

designed for the hard surfaces he's training on, tempting the fates by using a body not constructed for what he's doing, in a sense he is courting disaster by asking for an injury. There are so many factors that can cause injuries that it is difficult for a runner to avoid them all.

For example, any abrupt change in running habits can lead to trouble. Injuries can result from moving from an inactive schedule to an active one (such as laying off in the winter but plunging in when the weather is more conducive to jogging); moving from relatively low mileage to high mileage training (common among people preparing for their first marathon only weeks before the event); changing from long, slow distance to sprint activity; moving off the flat surfaces onto hill training (the kind of activity that has ended amateur running careers); moving from grass or campacted dirt to the streets and highways; moving from flat running shoes to the spiked variety (guaranteed to tear up the toes); changing from old to new shoes (or allowing well-worn shoes to continue wearing down until weight distribution is uneven); and — one of the biggest miseries of all — moving from the comfort of workouts to the stress of competitive racing.[9]

It is tempting to overwhelm running buffs with lists of the injuries created by running itself. However, in the name of fairness, it must be said that running can also contribute immeasurable benefits to the musculoskeletal system *if handled correctly*. But we are concerned here with incorrect handling. *We are looking at abuse and overuse*. We are looking at what happens to a runner moving from gentle jogging to the mania of competitive racing; we're looking at running that becomes more than an exercise. Unfortunately, the racer is beginning to predominate; the difficulty is in balance, or the lack of it. Moderation is not a code word with the running subculture.

Shoes have considerable impact on the number and severity of running injuries. How important are shoes? *Runner's World* magazine devotes an entire issue (October of each year) to the various shoes that are on the market. The magazine's staff, together with physiologists, physical education specialists, and experienced runners, rank the shoes according to utility. Most of the shoe companies vie for the honor of being placed high on the list of recommended designs. It takes no imagination to figure out that a high ranking in *Runner's World* is like money in the bank; it means increased sales in a very lucrative market where prices continue to swell (anywhere from $15 to $50).

What makes a good shoe? What makes a bad shoe? What is the difference between the two, and will that difference make a difference when it comes to injuries? The answer is a resounding *yes*. A bad shoe is worse than no shoe at all, based on the simplistic idea that a barefoot runner wouldn't run far enough or long enough on hard surfaces to do any real damage. A shoe, believe it or not, is not a running shoe because it has fancy stripes, a radial tire design on the tread, or comes in fashion-coordinated colors. It takes solid design and even better construction to make a real running shoe. Better yet, it takes some real thought as to what an individual runner will be doing with that particular shoe.

Every runner has a different kind of foot (or even feet), requiring running shoes that fit properly if the runner is to avoid debilitating injuries. Making an overall judgment on a single manufacturer's shoe is unfair to the manufacturer as well as to the runner considering a new pair of shoes.

There are, however, certain generalizations that must be made about any one running shoe, and it all comes down to fit. But fit is multifaceted in itself. There are many areas of fit to a shoe. If the toes are jammed, or too loose, either end of that spectrum, the runner will develop problems that lead to injuries. The most noticeable, but not the most serious by any means, is that of blue or black toes. This comes from bleeding beneath the nails and, together with the eventual loss of the affected nails, is so common among joggers that it is hardly noticed when runners get together.

Another crucial area of fit is ankle depth. How does

the foot fit into the back of the shoe? Does it move around or is the ankle snug? What about the heel counter, the part of the shoe that rides just under the heel and has to absorb tremendous shock from the pavement below? If that's too soft or too hard, the runner will begin to experience problems with his feet and ankles.

How are the shoes put together? Are they sewn or glued, or a combination of both? Do the shoes wear excessively fast, allowing the runner to become off-balance, creating a dangerous opportunity for injury?

In 1967, there were basically four brands of shoes to choose from: Adidas, Tiger, New Balance and Puma. Now there are dozens of shoes, including very inexpensive ones sold in discount stores. These *look* like running shoes but are really made-over, all-purpose sneakers with nothing more in common with a running shoe than a flashy stripe or two and a mazelike tread design having absolutely nothing to do with performance or wear.

Discount shoes will destroy a runner before he knows what's happening. Why? The shoes that are made to copy running shoes are not designed to take into account the terrific pressures and forces placed upon the running body, especially the lower body. Moreover, these cheap shoes can't protect the runner from hard surfaces that abound in this country. The cheap shoes can't adjust to stress and thus pass the burden on directly to the runner's aching body. A runner with cheap shoes asks for problems.

An increase in mileage is what puts any shoe to its greatest test. As the number of miles goes up, the shoe is put to more and more use, and any flaws show up quickly.

Shoes, as we have outlined, play an important role in helping to keep the runner healthy enough to come back for more punishment. The amount of running and where that running is done also contribute to the injury syndrome. But there are other factors to consider.

Warming up is imperative. We all know that, but we don't all do it. Warming up is the preparation of the body for exercise. In addition to giving the body a chance to make the adjustment from sedentary activity to strenuous activity, warm-up exercises will prevent some injuries.[10] Running tends to develop some muscles to the detriment of others; for example, back muscles can be strengthened considerably by a regular running program; in contrast, the abdominal muscles aren't worked as hard and so fall behind in development. This can create a type of over-compensation that often leads to an injury. How important is warm-up time? Very. If you look around at joggers taking off every day from their homes and trotting blissfully down the streets of America, you can bet that most of them did some toe-touching, or maybe a half-dozen jumping jacks, and that was it. If you're a runner, ask yourself how many times you've run without even stretching one muscle before commencing the workout. Embarrassing, isn't it?

Most experienced runners recommend ten to twelve minutes of *stretching exercises* that gently pull and push muscles, tendons and joints into more pliability. Some experienced runners such as Dr. George Sheehan and *Runner's World* founder and publisher Bob Anderson offer a series of exercises that prepare the anatomy for the stress of running. And after a workout there's a need for cooling down with additional stretching. Yes, more stretching, to insure that the mileage didn't create the overcompensation that can lead directly to injury. All runners who have been damaged by a lack of stretching will admit to being aware of the need for exercises. It seems to be a question of investment — both emotionally and from the aspect of time — that keeps many runners from doing what is necessary to avoid an injury.

How many runners are willing to put that much time and energy into stretching? It's hard to tell, but the number of injuries extant seem to indicate that the precept is violated more than it should be for the information available and understood. My survey of 100 middle-aged male runners in Oregon (who averaged five miles a day and had been running about four years) showed that 71 per cent suffered injuries from running, with 42 per cent being foot problems and 40 per cent leg problems (including those

92

fragile knees that take such a beating when we run). The respondents replied in sufficient numbers (almost four out of every ten) that running without proper warmup was a real danger to new joggers. Add these figures to the 5 per cent who felt that the right shoes were absolutely essential to running injury-free and you have an overwhelming move toward the problems that seem to plague runners.

The exercise routine is important as mileage increases. The shoes chosen by the runner to cover his tender feet are critical as mileage goes up. Mileage, mileage, and more mileage — and the injuries follow close behind like a shadow over the runner. What is clear at this point is that running is a healthful activity in concept, a pleasant form of exercise. However, what's not very clear is just how much running is healthful and just how much running is too much — and unhealthy.

How do you know when the mileage is piling up? When do you turn your back on the magazines and books that extol the heavenly virtues of mile after mile? Buried beneath the pictures of pretty people running in Central Park, the champions hunched over their cups of Gatorade after finishing a marathon, and the thin, nearly emaciated regulars basking in the sun of some faraway running paradise, is the short article on overuse, the problems that arise from too much, too far, and much too often.

Joggers seem to be interested in improving their physical fitness (at least that's what we tell each other when we have the chance). And, like everything else in our modern American society, we want the benefits instantly and without too many complications. But that leads to problems. Joe Henderson writes in *Jog, Run, Race,* "Most runners start in a sudden explosion of enthusiasm and not by a rational, conservative plan. Some of them get hurt."[11]

Runners by nature believe that running itself involves some discomfort and pain. After all, where would bodybuilders be without morning stiffness, football players without Monday stiffness, and so on? There are people who strongly believe that if an exercise doesn't hurt or if you're not sore the next day, it hasn't really done much good. Most high school coaches lodged in my memory approached athletics from that narrow point of view, and the idea seems to have slopped over into the running phenomenon, exacerbating the problem of overuse.

Overuse is just that — too much use of the body. It is the incomplete recovery of the body from an exercise routine. Some runners are able to push themselves day in and day out with little or no ill effects. They are the exceptions and impossible to explain. However, many runners need some time off between workouts to insure *complete recovery* and a fresh beginning before the next session.

There are a number of conditions which tell runners that they're into the overuse danger zone. *Mild leg soreness* is one symptom which is often overlooked or taken for granted. Many times the jogger will find his legs sore when he's ready for the next workout. This means that the legs haven't recovered sufficiently from the last time around the block. It is at this stage that injuries can occur. This is not to say the runner should *not* run that day, but that he should run *easily,* perhaps not as far or as fast as planned.

When I ran in the twenty-four-hour relay requiring fast mile runs at intervals approximately forty to forty-five minutes apart (twenty-six miles in twenty-four hours), my preparation had been so hasty (lack of speed work), that my body was not prepared for so many quick runs. The result was soreness that lasted off and on for nearly two months! It was definitely an indication of abuse and overuse of a body conditioned to run long, slow miles, and not fast miles over a long period. My price was paid.

Lowered general resistance to colds, headaches, fever blisters, and influenza-type sickness is also an indication of overuse. Some runners experience an increase in the sniffles when they're pushed too hard. One marathoner comes down with a heavy cold after every event.

A case of the blahs — that washed-out feeling associated with an "I-don't-give-a-darn" attitude — is the mind's way of telling the body that enough is enough. This overuse

95

measurement, if heeded, alerts the runner to cut down the number and duration of his workouts. Beginning runners with a case of the blahs, not realizing it's a symptom, often give up running entirely. What they don't know is that a reduction in their training program and not a total cessation is the answer.

Poor coordination, becoming a stumbling, bumbling fool, is sometimes an overuse indicator. The body seems to refuse to cooperate. What is actually happening is that the edge is eroding and general fatigue is entering the picture. This fatigue is translated into clumsiness and a decrease in coordination.

I've suffered from this problem myself. I've run into fire hydrants, tripped over ridiculously low curbs, and stumbled over lawn sprinklers. (The last of these helped me to throw a knee out of whack, creating back pains.) What should have been nothing more than some easy mid-course running corrections turned into a major problem; the hydrants, curbs and sprinklers are all a part of my regular journey — only when overuse sets in do they become formidable obstacles.

A kind of hangover from the previous workout is an overuse syndrome that touches on the washed-out feeling and lowered general resistance to illness. This "hangover" is a feeling that you just didn't recover from the previous workout. Sometimes this can be run off by taking to the streets anyway. More times than not, however, it can't be solved so easily. You've just had it for a while and rest is required for the comeback [12]

If you look at all five overuse indicators, you'll find one factor in common: stress. The reaction of the body to overstressing is what you face on those days when running is a supreme effort, if not a downright grind, that seems unworthy of being called an exercise. How do runners cope with overuse and the body's reaction to too much stress? Not very well. Most runners, especially beginners and those recently hooked on competitive racing, ignore most of the dangers from overuse. They feel it's natural to hurt a little (or even a lot, depending on their frame of mind and the amount of brainwashing they've received from books and magazines). Feeling washed-out is rarely associated with their running program. The sniffles hardly ever stand in a dedicated runner's way of another stiff workout. And being tired from yesterday's run is never given a second thought. But injury — debilitating, frustrating and lasting — can follow close behind.

According to an article in *Runner's World*, "The Six in Ten Who Break Down," your chances of having an injury which curtails your running for the year are almost two in three — more so if you're a teen-ager, a woman, or cover at least fifty miles per week. The article projects the idea that these figures only reflect chronic injuries.

For example, severe blisters and temporary muscle stiffness are not part of these statistics or the numbers would be higher.[13]

Chronic stress injuries (such as tendinitis and chondromalacia) that require the runner either to cut down his program drastically or actually stop running for periods of time (and perhaps undergo medical treatment such as the dreaded cortisone shots or other forms of painkillers) are numerous and should be taken seriously. Let's explore the factors that play a part in such injuries.

Age: There seems to be an idea around that children are really little exercise machines that can run all day without any severe problems developing. This may be true if you're just talking about play, where running is sporadic and mixed with other forms of movement. However, when our exploration turns to intensive or competitive running, it's nonsense to believe that a child cannot be injured by excessive mileage.

According to *Runner's World,* the highest injury rate of any age group is that in the nineteen-year-old and under category. The norm here is 60 per cent injury in a year's time. However, this group can run an injury rate of 72 per cent or better.[14] Young runners aren't prone to pay any particular attention to the warning signs discussed earlier. They are in a hurry to compete and eagerly take on the challenge of heavy mileage and fast pacing. These youngsters enter events one after another regardless of recovery and any overuse symptoms. They can be running maniacs. For the anxious youngster, training becomes as much competition as racing.

Running is dangerous — at any age — with the wrong attitude. Middle-aged runners can be seriously injured by taking on a very heavy program. Accurate statistics on the injury rate of middle-aged joggers are difficult to pin down, but it has become increasingly clear that a price is being paid by the man or woman who takes up jogging *after years of inactivity.* Warning: the middle-aged, weekend runner can disappear from the scene faster than most.

Sex: Women are vulnerable. They have some special problems that even they themselves would prefer to ignore.[15] Secondary amenorrhea, or the loss of normal menses, can be experienced by women runners who pare down to a running weight that's too light for normal body interaction. Cases have been reported of women who dropped below desirable weight and began to have trouble with their menstruation. The problem is that running introduces a loss of weight if the runner becomes so enamored with the exercise that all personal habits become involved. Many times a female runner hooked on the competitive aspect will not only run enough to burn substantial calories, but she'll reduce her intake of high-calorie foods and lose even more weight. There's also evidence that heavy running can place stress on the pituitary gland, and the menses in turn will suffer.[16]

There are also questions about the effects of running during pregnancy. Many runners claim that pregnant women can run right up until giving birth, but this is yet to be proved on a statistical basis and has to be suspect.

The final point to consider is that of sexual differences in cultural activity. Dr. Joan Ullyot, herself a fine runner, explains:

> When women start to run, both physique and society-influenced life-style cause them more difficulties than male runners. The troubles are not due to inborn sex differences so much as the fact that most women never run after ages ten to twelve. We see similar injuries in older men who start running after years of inactivity. It's just that women reach the point of atrophy at age twenty, men at age forty.[17]

Surface: Grass and dirt don't protect runners as much as first thought, yet hard surfaces are *absolutely detrimental* over a long period of time. According to Dr. Roger H. Michael, Chief of Orthopedic Surgery at Union Memorial Hospital in Baltimore, and a member of the College of Sports Medicine, hard surfaces break down the body's muscles. Dr. Michael feels that the uninitiated too often buy a poorly constructed pair of inexpensive tennis shoes and start running on hard surfaces, such as the street.

100

This leads to such injuries as plantar fascitis (inflammation of the arch) and the infamous shin splints.[18]

Dr. Robert Kerlan of the National Health Institute and an orthopedic consultant for several major league baseball teams claims that the softer the surface beneath your feet, the less chance of sustaining a jogging-related injury. Grass is best, then dirt, and last is pavement.

Mileage: This is the killer from a figurative point of view. When running tops fifty miles per week, the injuries climb to 73 per cent; that is, more than seven out of every ten runners covering fifty or more miles per week can expect some type of debilitating injury sometime during their career. Compare that figure with only 34 per cent for those running twenty-five miles or less per week.[19] The difference is more than double.

Racing or competition also increases injuries, due to the strain placed on the entire body from pushing for extremes. Usually, however, mileage is a part of this problem too, as competition demands additional mileage that climbs above the average (or at least above the injury prone fifty-miles-per-week level), to insure some kind of competitive condition.

Therefore, *who is most vulnerable on a composite basis?* The answer is a female, nineteen years or younger, running on a hard surface, and putting in fifty or more miles per week. She's probably competing on a regular basis too, as high schools are now creating running programs for women on an ever-increasing basis.

This doesn't leave the rest of us who are not young, female, or running competitively entirely safe. Young males are almost as prone to injuries as young females. The difference is in what Joan Ullyot claims is the late start women have in running, due to sexual discrimination.

It should be marked at this point that injuries can come *at all levels, to all types of runners.* Chronic complaints cut across the grain of all who take part in steady jogging. Laurence Morehouse says that there may be no way to avoid jogging injuries.[20] I have to agree. My first thirty-six months of running gave me twenty months of painful injuries. My problems stemmed from too many miles, too fast, too soon, and, for a while, a very inexpensive pair of shoes that nearly cost me all of my toenails and both ankles. I, too, learned the hard way.

NOTES FROM CHAPTER FOUR

1. Laurence Morehouse and Leonard Gross, *Total Fitness In 30 Minutes A Week* (New York: Simon & Schuster, 1976), pp. 201-202.
2. Joel Henning, "The Simple Truth About Blisters," *Runner's World*, September 1978, pp. 36-41.
3. George Sheehan, *Encyclopedia of Athletic Medicine* (Mountain View, California: World Publications, 1972), p. 31.
4. Ibid., p. 31.

5. Ibid., p. 31.

6. Ibid., p. 31.

7. Ibid., p. 31.

8. *Runner's World*, p. 38.

9. *Runner's World* editors, *Athlete's Feet* (Mountain View, California: World Publications, 1974), pp. 36-37.

10. Lance, *Running For Health and Beauty*, p. 104.

11. Joe Henderson, *Jog, Run, Race* (Mountain View, California: World Publications, 1977), p. 3.

12. Long-time runner Tom Osler's symptoms of overuse. *Runner's World* editors, *The Complete Runner* (New York: Avon Books, 1974), pp. 100-105.

13. Dr. Joan Ullyot, "Six in Ten Who Break Down," *Runner's World* December 1975, pp. 34-35.

14. Ibid., p. 35.

15. See G. J. Erdelyi's "Effects of Exercise on the Menstrual Cycle," *The Physician and Sportsmedicine*, March 1976, and Christine E. Haycock and Joan Gillette's "Susceptibility of Women Athletes to Injury," *Journal of the American Medical Association*, 12 July 1976.

16. Leon Speroff, "Is Jogging Harmful to a Woman's Health?" *Northwest Magazine, Portland Oregonian*, 27 November 1977.

17. Dr. Joan Ullyot, "Six in Ten Who Break Down," *Runner's World*, December, 1975, p. 37.

18. Interview with Dr. Roger H. Michael, "Your Summer Sports: Just How Dangerous?" *U.S. News and World Report*, 31 July 1978, p. 21.

19. Dr. Joan Ullyot, "Six in Ten Who Break Down," *Runner's World*, December 1975, p. 35.

20. Laurence Morehouse and Leonard Gross, *Maximum Performance* (New York: Simon & Schuster, 1977), p. 327.

An excellent approach to the injuries associated with running and their aftermath is Mark Williams's "Fighting Chondromalacia," *Runner's World*, October 1976.

103

CHAPTER FIVE: MARATHONS OR MAYHEM?

"'By this time, none of us was running a race.
We were trying to help one another survive an
ordeal. There was no loneliness among the
long-distance runners.'"

Joe Falls
The Boston Marathon

Nothing seems to sum up the attitude of runners toward their chosen exercise more than the simple idea that if some running is good (granted), more has to be better (not necessarily). And a lot more must be the best of all. This means that running not only becomes addictive, it begins to grow geometrically until one day it is time to go after the absolute prize of them all: a marathon — 26 miles, 385 yards, 11 inches.

Marathon running is a genuine phenomenon. It is unquestionably one of the greatest feats ever to take athletics by storm since goldfish swallowing went out with the Great Depression. If you run any distance at all — whether it be a couple of times a week or a couple of times per month — sooner or later your fancy will turn to the magic miles of marathoning and a whole new vista will open up.

Marathons have always been popular. We've had dance marathons, swim marathons (Florence Chadwick attacking the cold, dark English Channel, for example), and the Indianapolis 500, a different type of marathon for man and machine, every spring. However, nothing has quite caught the fancy of the ordinary mortal as the 26-plus-mile run. It wasn't always 26 miles and 385 yards — it was around 24 miles until the Olympic Games of 1908, when the royal family of England wanted the race to start on the grounds of their residence. The race went from that point to the stadium at White City, a distance of 26 miles, 385 yards, 11 inches. The standard stuck and from then on, people have been huffing and puffing over 26.2 miles in such places as Boston, Chicago, New York, and at the plains of Marathon where the Greeks started it centuries ago. (History's first marathoner was Pheidippides, running 40 kilometers with the Greek equivalent of a telegram for the war effort.)

Why do people push their tired, aching and numb bodies

over such a vast distance? Many reasons. One that stands above the others is the idea that running a marathon is the ultimate personal test against time, distance, fatigue and oneself. What more could be asked from a single event?

Let's face it — you have to be a little crazy and a whole lot courageous to want to run a marathon. You have to be a little mad to want to do *anything* that requires anywhere from a little over two hours (if you are Bill Rodgers or Frank Shorter) to five hours (if you have to walk quite a bit). Either way, the 26 miles and 385 yards can turn into an agonizing time and personal torment.

Reasons? Dr. Thaddeus Kostrubala claims that running marathons helps us to blast out of our twentieth century world and integrate with a far more primitive animal.

In other words, marathons may well be a link with the past when life was simpler and certainly less confusing. Running a marathon could be putting the runner in touch with his basic instincts.

But why, the question persists, run a marathon? Ten or twelve miles could do the job if running distance is what counts. What's so magical about twenty-six and a fraction miles? That is as hard to answer as why men tackle certain mountains time and time again, no matter how many times the peak has been scaled before their attempt. It is just there. *It exists to be conquered.*

More and more people are now taking to the streets

to run a marathon. In 1978, approximately 200 major marathons were run; 40,000 or more people went the legendary distance. Ten years ago the figure couldn't have been above 3,000. The increase in first-time runners is staggering. Every race brings out young and old to meet the challenge that tests men's will to beat the unbeatable.

When marathoners are asked what they think about when they run the distance, some of the responses suggest that the numbness goes beyond arms and legs. "I don't think I was thinking," is one reply. "Ask me in a month," is another. One marathoner responded with "Because they're there. It's a test. A challenge. From the waist down, I hurt. I'm glad I'm through." Some think about how bad they really feel: "The farther out I get, the worse I feel and the more I think about myself."[1]

Some runners compete in a marathon with only the end in sight. They are merely hoping to finish the grueling race. "I admired it. You know, I don't know why I did it. I wanted to see if I could. My main objective is to finish." What about being able to outshine your friends and neighbors? "Like a mountain, it's there. It's something to do. Just the satisfaction of doing it. Not many people can."[2]

Sometimes, and now we're bordering on a little amateur psychology, a marathon is used as a surrogate for all those areas of life that seem frustrating and without real meaning for the individual. It's the completion of a difficult com-

108

mitment that doesn't take years to accomplish. A couple of hours or more and you're suddenly through with the dream for this time around. It's done. In most of our daily activities we're frustrated; in running we can get from one point to another point and we've done it; it's satisfying that way.[3]

Can the pain of marathoning actually be a pleasure? "I'm sure it was (fun), but I've got a theory that pain and pleasure are the same; in pain you feel pleasure."[4]

Where does that leave our inquiry? Running a marathon is fun. Running a marathon is pain. Running a marathon is done because it's there. Running a marathon makes you better than the next guy. It can even make you immortal.[5]

Is marathoning an obsession that can be avoided by those who take up the art of gentle jogging with very little thought of entering the world of distance competition? Should the marathon be avoided? My answer is *yes* on both counts!

Before we investigate the dangers associated with running more than twenty-six miles, let us look at the people who run marathons on a regular basis and examine how they feel about their accomplishments. First of all, it will do little good in our search for answers to talk with "professionals" such as Frank Shorter or Bill Rodgers. In fact, most running literature is replete with quotes, training schedules and diets of the top American marathon runners.

Instead, we must look at Joe Jogger, the week-end marathoner who moves up from jogging a few miles a day to take on his first bona fide 26-mile, 385-yard-jaunt over the streets and highways of Anytown, U.S.A.

Running a marathon, if you weren't aware of it by now, takes a heck of a lot of conditioning, much courage and a little luck. The training is obvious. You have to run the *practice* miles before tackling the *real* miles of a marathon. If the body is unprepared to fight its way through hours of stress, the marathon experience turns into one of despair and sometimes tragedy. People have died running a marathon. We'll explore that unfortunate avenue later.

Courage is easy to see too. When the pain mounts, it takes personal courage not to chuck the whole effort and hitch a ride to the finish line. It's done all the time. Scores of people fail to finish the Boston Marathon every April. Most of them were probably unprepared for the grueling test of mind and body, and tried to "gut" their way through the miles. Some hit the "wall" around twenty miles. This is a kind of barrier that runners have created. It does have a physiological basis for some runners, however, as twenty miles is where a lot of runners begin to dehydrate if they haven't carefully managed their fluid intake during the early part of the race.

Finally, luck comes into the picture. Who can predict the weather, or if air pollution will knock you off at fifteen

110

miles by choking up your lungs? What about a tiny spot on a toe that rubs raw with each passing mile and finally become so large that it is a bloody mass of tangled tissue that stops you dead in your tracks? What about starting off too fast, an easy thing to do because of the intense excitement and tension surrounding a race that usually draws thousands of runners from all over the nation, and then finding yourself in trouble near the end?

Luck comes into play because there are so many factors that can reduce a marathoner to dust over the long course. We know that heat or cold can destroy a runner on any given day. We know from experience that dehydration can spell finis to a runner who seems to be doing fine. We also know what happens to a runner who happens to get too close to a car, something that's possible in a major marathon where miles and miles of roads have to be policed and carefully controlled. At best, a marathon runner will swallow a lot of pollutants from cars cruising too close to the marathon course.

A marathon is not an art form. It's a war against man's fragile body and sensitive soul. No one who has run a marathon forgets that ecstatic feeling at the finish. Just knowing that it's over, that the pain will stop, coupled with the knowledge that *you've actually made it* — somehow crossed twenty-six miles of ground on foot — can be very near a religious experience![6]

Joe Falls of the *Detroit Free Press* has caught the atmosphere of the marathon experience in his lively book *The Boston Marathon*. Joe covered the 1976 Boston Marathon and found:

> So it's really not who wins. It's the people in the race. Big people. Little people. White people. Red people. Black people. Yellow people. Men people. Women people. Boy people. Girl people. And dogs. It's a fact that each April, on the 19th day of the month, these people – doctors, lawyers, plumbers, carpenters, clerks, bookkeepers, soldiers, cops, mill hands, steelworkers, bricklayers, bill collectors, hairdressers, milkmen, students, husbands, wives, lovers – even the unemployed and those who don't have lovers – gather on that village green in Hopkinton to begin The Great Adventure. They hope to go the full distance – 26 miles, 385 yards – and experience that sweet feeling of success, crossing the finish line in front of the Big Pru. Maybe it's three o'clock. Maybe it's four o'clock. Maybe it's six o'clock and everyone has gone home. But if the Boston Marathon is about anything at all, it's about finishing: to conquer one's self.[7]

Marathon means pain. It would be sheer folly to see the experience as a pleasant stroll that takes anywhere from two to five hours. Thaddeus Kostrubala writes that the marathon is impossible, both physically and spiritually. He's afraid of it. He disdains driving the course ahead of time for fear of discouraging himself. And yet in 1974 he ran the Honolulu Marathon. He describes his finish over three and a half hours after starting:

> There are crowds of people the last mile on either side. No one knows me, but they applaud as I finish. They do that for everyone. God, it feels great! I am all alone. My back straightens and I feel lighter and I come into the finish smiling, actually grinning. At the last 200 yards I begin to sprint. God knows where I get this energy, but it feels right.
>
> My feelings are so strong these last 200 yards that I begin to choke up, to feel that inner urge to cry. Like a kid. I know I can't do that; maybe I can, but it would look odd. All these emotions come boiling up and then, before I know it, I cross the finish line in the crowd of other finishers, their families and friends.
>
> I have finished: I have won. [8]

Marathoning is addictive. The feelings connected with running such a distance with thousands of other people intent on survival can't be dismissed merely as part of the pursuit of fitness for fitness' sake. They can't be equated with concern for arteries, and aren't a natural development from taking up jogging to lose a little weight. Marathoning is part madness, collective as well as singular, and absolutely captivating for anyone who even begins to wonder what it would be like to cross that finish line smiling and crying at the same time, while the body screams that "enough is

113

enough."

Be warned: Watch your first marathon from the sidelines. See the runners close up, smell the excitement in the air, share the success and the heartbreak, and you'll be filling out that entry form for the next marathon in your area. It *can* happen that way. It is just that addictive.

Yet pain continues to surface over and over when we look at the marathon's lure. To hurt enough to run because the pain is there and something to be conquered is one aspect of the phenomenon.

> The pain in a marathon's closing stages can be so great as to *force* meaning upon the run. Men submit to the ordeal not in spite of the pain but because of it . . . The distance and discomfort already endured scream that this must not be for nothing, so you go on. Afterward, in the dressing room, men hang stiffly on one another, too exhausted to untie their shoes . . . [9]

The difference between a mile and the marathon is the difference between being burned with a match and being slowly roasted over hot coals. But a miracle occurs when the marathon is over and a beatific calm settles over the runner. No matter how extreme the torture, it seems to be worth every gut ache, every leg cramp, and every blister.[10]

Is marathoning really a dangerous exercise? Of course

it is dangerous, very dangerous. We know what it means to run a marathon — at least what it means to those who run and finish the grind. But what does it mean if you're one of the unlucky runners who can't cope with the hardship? A runner whose body simply fails to appreciate the conquest of itself and breaks down somewhere between the hope-filled beginning and the pain-filled conclusion?

The serious problems connected with marathon running can be broken down into two categories. First, there's the problem of running in a race when you're *not actually prepared* for what's ahead. Second, there's the problem of taking part in a race where you are biomechanically *not suited* for the conditions that will be imposed on the body. There's probably a third category here, too, one that's not as readily recognized as the other two. This is the area of competition, the problem of taking part in a competition when you're really not of a competitive nature.

Training for a marathon is very serious business. Don't let anyone tell you that running a few soft miles a day, every day, before the big event will be enough to insure an injury-free time over the twenty-six miles. It just isn't so. For every runner who manages to scrape through with little previous preparation, there is a runner in difficulty throughout the race and in danger of being hurt.

Common *mistakes* made by runners who set out for the first time to conquer themselves and the marathon

115

distance include believing the following misconceptions:

Running is a real lark. Some runners believe that they can walk, run, skip and crawl their way over the marathon course and then be able to proudly announce that they made the Mt. Everest of running. True, some unthinking and carefree runners *have* made it over the distance without any preparation. However, the odds are against this kind of behavior. It is a foolhardy stunt, and nothing else.

You can make up in speed what you lack in training mileage; running makes it happen. *Lots* of running makes it happen more easily and with less chance of serious injury (bringing back our thesis that training mileage can be the cause of injuries too). Speed training — fast runs of short duration — will not prepare the average runner for the rigors of marathoning. The increased chances for injury are there.

Run the marathon in practice and then you'll feel confident it can be done on race day. This is a great way to come out with an injury. Too many marathon distances, too close together, can only lead to overuse and over-stressing. If you train for your marathon by running marathon distances, you *increase the odds* of a debilitating injury.

Keep training hard right up to race day and you'll be in shape for the grind ahead. The amount of stress placed on the body covering a marathon distance can't be measured.

116

It's *immense*. Some runners can recover overnight; others never quite recover for weeks or months afterward. However, by *cutting back* on training as the day approaches, you give the body an opportunity to prepare for the grueling race. This is just plain good sense.

Choose a marathon in the summer when it's nice and warm so that you'll be comfortable during the long hours it takes. After looking at what heat can do to a runner, anyone consciously choosing a warm, sunny day to conquer the first marathon is either crazy or ignorant (or both). *Heat and marathons don't mix.* It's proven every year.

Eat heartily before the race and you'll have plenty of energy. We all need energy to run twenty-six plus miles. However, reserves will not be drawn from something eaten just before racetime. The chances of gastrointestinal upset offset any benefits from eating so close to the start. This is an *individual situation,* though. Some runners can eat lightly right before a race and have no problems. Others, however, will find the burden of food too much and will end up off to the side, looking quite green at the gills.

Start quickly and you'll be able to coast when the going gets tough. The end of this should read "and not be able to finish." If you don't run *your* pace – a pace that you can hold comfortably mile in and mile out – the chances are you'll drop out before the end is in sight. Injuries are associated with fast pacing, as you are caught in a position where the body has been overstressed too soon and has to fight for its chance to recover.

Resume full training right after the marathon — this will give you a jump on what's coming next. If you're lucky enough to have survived the first marathon, your body needs time to rebuild itself. Cells, tissue, and muscles have been worn down trying to keep you going over all those miles. Immediate training can only *aggravate* any slight injury or create a whole new set of problems that will show up later. Stress fractures, as you remember, are most common when the body is in an overload situation.

Take in no liquids while you're in the marathon — that will save time and keep you from becoming sick. If you can stand the thirst generated by a dehydrating body (and some people can resist it), you are stronger than most runners. However, beyond the immediate discomfort, if the fluids lost during a race are not replaced *during the time they're being lost,* you run an excellent chance of becoming a victim of *heat stroke.* Runners lose a lot of weight during the marathon and almost all of it is precious body fluids. Running sans liquids is tantamount to suicide.[11]

These mistakes — arising primarily from a runner's taking the marathon too lightly or feeling too confident about his conditioning — are not the only pitfalls in marathon running. Biomechanically speaking, some people

118

are just not made to run 26.2 miles. If you are prone to tendinitis, bursitis, and some of the other ailments created by a tendency of the body to fight itself, you're going to run the high risk of increasing your injury rate. It's all wrapped up in the extra mileage. This goes for preparing yourself for the marathon and the actual marathon race over 26 miles, 385 yards, 11 inches. There is no hard data proving that everyone, no matter who they are, can safely engage in distance running as long as they work their mileage into marathon-style training. Everyone is not ready for bone-crushing football. Everyone is *not* ready for tissue-searing marathon running.

Fred Lebow of the New York Road Runners Club and race director for the New York City Marathon said: "In 1967, when I started running, there was no one to tell me what to do, no book to read. Now you can smother in literature, go deaf at running clinics. There is no excuse for a runner not being prepared. Even so, three of our entrants died between signing up in July and the race." *(Sports Illustrated,* October 30, 1978.)

The final issue here is competition. Some runners are strictly fun-runners, nothing else. Some make a competition out of every facet of life. And some people in both categories can't become caught up in the fever of racing without risking injury from the peculiar nature of competitive

119

running. Many injuries in sports, not just marathon running, occur because the noncompetitive athlete tries to compete with the real athletic warrior. It is said by many coaches that basketball, especailly professional basketball, is not an art but a war. Equally, marathon running is not a frolic in the woods but a deadly serious competition that tests the courage as well as the physical fitness of the players.

The question that you should ask yourself about marathoning is: Do I want to invest time, lots of energy, and the opportunity for a potential physical breakdown in conquering 26.2 miles, or do I just want the alleged benefits offered by gentle running?

When you move from a fitness program to marathon training, you move from a simple cost/benefit concept to the negative externality of ultradistance running. In simpler terms, when you increase from a couple of miles per day, a couple of days per week, as a fitness adjunct, to the rugged, almost torturous eight to ten miles per day, almost daily, to meet the demands of a marathon program, you're moving from mileage that provides benefits at some cost to ultramileage that can almost guarantee problem spinoffs. And when you're blinded by the almost obsessive drive connected with running the marathon, the choice isn't always clear.

Are marathons really that popular? Are we exploring a small, but highly visible phenomenon that has captured the attention of the media? Does it look bigger than it really is?

The influx of new marathoners each year is astonishing. A special program for the 1977 New York City Marathon published by the editors of the *New Times* magazine indicated nearly 4,300 entrants in this grueling citywide tour. The list, however, was incomplete. The magazine carried an apology to those who had entered too late to be included in the listing. The actual total was closer to 5,000 people ready to do battle with the streets of New York. But this was only the tip of the iceberg. The 1978 edition of the Big Apple race drew a crowd of 11,400. It was *the first time* that marathon entrants broke 10,000 in the United States and was a harbinger of things to come. The most significant part of this record-breaking traffic jam was that 42 per cent of the starters were lining up for their first marathon! How many finished? About 75 per cent, or 8,000 men, women and children, made it to the end.

The Boston Marathon annually draws thousands of runners, including over 3,000 unofficial entrants who either failed to qualify from a previous race or didn't complete the paper work soon enough. The managers of this highly publicized race have watched the entry list grow to a point where it is almost uncontrollable. In an attempt to keep the race manageable, they have set a qualification for the runners: a time in a previous official marathon of three hours for men under forty, and three hours, thirty minutes for women and all other men.[12]

Yet the numbers continue to grow, in spite of the qualifications needed. This means that unlike New York City, everyone lined up for the starter's pistol in Boston is supposed to have finished a previous marathon and run a respectable time of three to three and a half hours. Boston's monster crowd each April has already covered the 26.2 miles somewhere else and is back for more punishment. Indeed, there are so many starters that those in the back of the huge pack (seeded there by time — slower runners to the rear so that the swifties don't run them down in the first few miles) may actually have to wait a few minutes *after* the gun has been fired to start running. It takes that long for the entire behemoth to move out!

How many marathons are there? In 1978, approximately one hundred seventy major marathons were scheduled throughout the country (including Hawaii and Alaska). California, naturally, leads the way, with twenty-four different races over 26.2 miles.[13] Colorado supplies what is probably the most challenging — an agonizing run up Pike's Peak. The world's largest road race to date (1979) took place in Stramilano, Italy. Fifty thousand people entered the 22-kilometer run.

It doesn't take a fortune teller to predict the future of competitive running. Marathons will continue to grow in popularity. Marathoners will continue to grow in numbers. The running subculture will eventually see to that. Unfortunately, the injuries from running will continue to grow, and so will the number of deaths. *Running can kill* and the next chapter tells how.

NOTES FROM CHAPTER FIVE

1. Underhill, "Why Run The Marathon?" p. 20.
2. Ibid.
3. Ibid.
4. Ibid.
5. Marathoners can beat coronaries, according to cardiologist Thomas J. Bassler. Dr. Bassler claims that marathoners develop large hearts and collateral arteries, features that preclude the possibility of a fatal heart attack. Dr. Bassler is a regular contributor to the National Jogging Association's newspaper *The Jogger*. His thesis has been challenged by other heart specialists and has become suspect because of recent deaths among experienced runners.
6. Some runners actually cry for joy. The finish line of a marathon is a cross between a battlefield hospital and the ending of a religious pilgrimage.
7. Joe Falls, *The Boston Marathon* (New York: Macmillan Publishing Co., 1977), p. xii.
8. Thaddeus Kostrubala, *The Joy of Running* (New York: J. B. Lippincott, 1976), pp. 145-151.

9. *Runner's World, Complete Runner*, p. 19.

10. James F. Fixx, *The Complete Book of Running* (New York: Random House, 1977), p. 205.

11. Joe Henderson, ed., *The Complete Marathoner* (Mountain View, California: World Publications, 1978), pp. 113-116.
Fred Lebow, *Sports Illustrated* 30 October 1978.

12. There seems to be very little that will deter a marathoner out to make the qualifying time for Boston. Dennis Rainear finished the last sixteen miles of the Grand Valley Marathon in Allendale, Michigan, on November 4, 1978, with a .22 caliber bullet lodged in his head! He was accidentally shot while running the race. The shell flattened against his skull, nearly knocking Rainear off his feet, but he managed to finish the race in three hours, nine minutes. The bullet was then removed at Grand Rapids Butterworth Hospital. And, oh yes, he failed to make the qualifying time of three hours for the Boston Marathon.

13. Henderson, *Complete Marathoner*, pp. 387-395.

CHAPTER SIX: DEATH AT AN EARLY MILEAGE

"To us jogging is murder."

The Inner World of the Middle-
aged Man — Peter Chew

When anyone mildly interested in jogging brings up the sudden exercise death (SED) syndrome, most people connected with running and its explosive growth in this country begin to sneer and talk about other facets of running — mostly the good things associated with cardio-vascular exercise. Sudden exercise death is not one of the

125

more popular subjects in running magazines and other forms of literature available to the enthusiast.

Is running dangerous enough to kill someone outright? Can you actually die from too much running? We've explored the hazards that stem from being out on the streets with moving vehicles. We've looked at the specific problems that come from jogging where muggers like to hang out. We've probed heat stroke and hypothermia, and air pollution and how it may affect a runner's immediate health.

However, what we're exploring at this point is the connection between cardiac arrest from a strenuous activity that is alleged to bring near-immortality and the deaths that are occurring in the running community. This seems to be the paradox of running: death from an activity promoted to prevent death in the first place! Cardiac arrest is not one of the most talked-about areas in the dozens of running books crowding the stores, but it is a real problem.

Crashing airplanes and rampaging floods gain considerably more attention on the evening news than running deaths, but that doesn't mean that those deaths don't happen and that they don't need some explaining. On October 13, 1978, a story carried by most American newspapers opened up the question of whether running can kill. The article was headlined: "Marathoner's Death Sends

126

Tremor Through Runner's World."[1] Congressman Good-loe R. Byron died of an apparent heart attack while running along the Chesapeake and Ohio Canal near Washington, D.C.

What makes this report, one that shook the running community right down to its athletic socks, more than just "another" tragedy is that Representative Byron was not your typical jogger (and he certainly wasn't the stereotyped week-end warrior, overweight and underexercised). No, Goodloe R. Byron couldn't be singled out as one of those newcomers who probably would have died sooner if he hadn't taken up running before his fatal attack. Byron's death is not that easy to dismiss.

Byron was *not* overweight. He was *not* a sometime jogger trying to make up for lost years at the dinner table. Byron was one of the best, one that the running community could point to as a prime example of those things running can do for a person seriously interested in fitness. Representative Byron had run in six Boston Marathons and had a personal best time of three hours, twenty-eight minutes when he was forty-four years of age in 1974. He had run in seven JFK fifty-mile races, the ultradistance competition growing out of the overcrowded marathons. And, for the absolute purists, he hadn't touched a cigarette in twenty-five years!

According to a friend, Byron ran almost every day for at least thirty minutes. He had scheduled a mini-marathon

127

for the middle of October in celebration of National Jogging Day.

In short, Goodloe E. Byron was everything that a running enthusiast could boast of when talking about the benefits accruing to a middle-aged runner. And yet, he died of heart failure at age forty-eight.

Recently two veteran runners died within minutes of each other in the most bizarre of circumstances. The two men, one aged forty-eight and the other sixty-one, were out jogging together when the younger man collapsed. When the sixty-one-year-old ran for help, he too collapsed. The two men died *within five minutes of each other* at a local hospital.[2]

In 1977, Henry Jordan, former Green Bay Packers football star, and a man who kept himself in reasonably sound condition off the playing field, died of a heart attack while jogging at the Milwaukee Athletic Club. Jordan was only forty-two years old.

In April of 1977, the tennis world was stunned by news of the untimely death of thirty-year-old Karen Krantzcke of Australia. She had just won a doubles final in Tallahassee, Florida. Ms. Krantzcke decided that her cooling-off period would include a short jog. This is probably one of the most common ways to gear down after a competitive match. The tennis star collapsed two hundred yards from the tennis court. There was no warning. She died of heart failure.

The running community was shocked and dismayed when a very experienced runner from a suburb of Oakland, California, died during a morning jog in July 1976. His name was Jim Shettler and he was only forty-two years old when the end came on the streets of Pleasant Hill where he had run many times before.[3] Jim Shettler was a runner's runner in the sense that he put in a lot of miles and had been competing a long time before his sudden death. He had attempted several marathons but had never finished one because he usually ran too fast at the start. The day before he died, Jim Shettler had run twenty-three miles in practice, the longest continuous run of his career. He had been running most of his adult life, setting records for the mile and 3000-meter steeplechase as a student at San Francisco State College. Only a few months before his death he had captured the National AAU Masters 25-kilometer championship. The Master class contains runners over the age of forty. According to reports, Jim Shettler died of a massive heart attack.

Dr. Leslie Truelove, who had taken up running six years earlier, collapsed at the 21-mile mark of the Lion's Gate International Marathon. One of his arteries had given out. Death was inevitable. He was forty-seven.[4]

Donald Palmer, a forty plus member of the Corona del Mar Track Club, was found dead in his car at a shopping center. He had died of an apparent heart attack.[5]

129

Despite such incidents, runners continue to believe that they are immune from what happened to Henry Jordan, Jim Shettler and others. Yet the list of fatalities grows each year. One of the unfortunate parts of compiling the runner's obituary is that most such deaths never make headlines because the jogger has no reputation to make the story newsworthy beyond the local scene. But how many Jim Shettlers are there who go out for a morning run and never make it back to their homes alive? How many Henry Jordans collapse while working out in gyms? And how many Donald Palmers are there who are runners by nature and yet die behind the wheel of a parked car, felled by a massive heart attack?

Such tragedies will continue to occur as more and more runners *without proper precautions and a healthy respect for the hazards* take to the streets of this country in an attempt to borrow on their future.

Not all doctors are convinced that jogging is the only answer to what may ail you. In fact, not all doctors are convinced that jogging is *any* answer to what may ail you. Dr. Irving Levetos in *You Can Beat The Odds On A Heart Attack* points out directly, "Ready to rush out and run a mile? Don't. Exercise can kill you."[6] William Fossbender writes in *You and Your Health,* "Many [people] suffer heart attacks jogging."[7]

130

Probably one of the most devastating attacks on jogging ever made by the medical community came from two cardiologists in the San Francisco Bay area. Doctors Meyer Friedman and Ray Rosenman, in their highly acclaimed book *Type A Behavior and Your Heart,* zero in on jogging with a passion not usually aimed at the running community. These heart specialists leave little doubt as to where they place jogging, the latest exercise craze. First, they are against strenuous exercise of *any type* that can push the heart *to a limit.* Each of us has a limit but sometimes where that critical point resides is beyond our control and even our knowledge. The doctors feel that everyone *past the age of thirty-five* should avoid pushing to the limit with any exercise that creates stress, and "first on our blacklist is jogging." Further, they believe that this "miserable post-collegiate athletic travesty" has killed hundreds of Americans.[8]

Type A Behavior and Your Heart left an impression on many people who read the book not so much for the heavy criticism that was leveled at strenuous exercise (and especially jogging, since it does receive the most criticism by name), but for the concept that certain personality traits (continual dissatisfaction with achievements, extremely competitive) create a heart-attack-prone person. These traits have quite a lot in common with those of the very competitive runner! These people are called *type A*

131

by Rosenman and Friedman, as opposed to *type B,* the easygoing, relaxed person who isn't interested in setting new records each week.

Before dismissing these two cardiologists as just two more antijogging doctors, keep in mind that many competitive runners are definitely type A people. If we look at the situation from this perspective, it isn't hard to see that running could be very dangerous for these people. And the worst part of it is that they aren't the least bit aware of the potential hazard.

The major problem associated with running and the possibility of a heart attack is that of hidden heart disease. This is not something that a runner can detect on his own. However, a stress test administered by a physician can reveal defects or damage. This is an examination of the heart's efficiency while the subject is stressing. It's a kind of look at the heart as it is performing under pressure. It can be done while the subject is running on a treadmill or riding a bicycle fixed to the floor, but the treadmill is best. While the exerciser is moving on the treadmill, his heart is monitored through an electrocardiogram. The EKG will indicate any abnormalities and the doctor in charge can terminate the test if he feels the subject is in immediate danger or if the subject complains of discomfort. The rate of pace (how fast the treadmill revolves) and the incline (the slant of the treadmill plane) are gradually increased throughout the test until the exerciser is at maximum performance.

Why is such a stress test important? If you're thinking of taking up running and you're over thirty, or haven't exercised very much in preceding years, or if you're overweight or a smoker (or all of these), the test can give a good indication of your limitations. Sometimes, and this is very important, the test can show that a full running program is *not advisable for you* and that you would be taking your life out on the streets if the results of the test were ignored.

But despite their benefits, the use of stress tests is not widespread. And that's the rub. My survey, for example, indicated that out of eighty active, middle-aged male runners – men who were running around five miles per day – only 16.7 per cent had had a stress test before starting to run hard. In other words, only about thirteen men out of eighty who had taken up running in their middle years had been cleared for the exercise, with the stress test as the important back-up information. Moreover, out of the thirteen who had the stress test, only five had ever gone back for an updating!

And I'm no better. I went back to running after a layoff of nearly eighteen years. In three years I've racked up close to five thousand miles (including many injury-ridden months). Did *I* have a stress test? No.

Another problem that may lead to sudden heart attacks and sudden exercise death (SED) is that of not watching for or heeding signals that the body gives as clear warnings that things are not going right. Who knows if these warnings were prevalent for Jim Shettler or the others who died suddenly?

Sometimes, however, a signal can be a normal, non-threatening response instead of a crucial indication of trouble. Chest discomfort and shortness of breath can be serious. However, chest discomfort can also be experienced in a race if the pace becomes heated and shortness of breath is not uncommon after a long sprint. If sudden fatigue seems intense, this could be another warning, but there are days when running is definitely a real chore and fatigue is the companion. It is imperative that every runner learn to read and evaluate the signals that his body sends, and a complete physical examination including a stress test can be an important aid in this learning process.

Illness is also a factor. For example, a bout of influenza can weaken a runner and leave him vulnerable to sudden and complete collapse. Medication too can disrupt body rhythms. For those who return to the streets too soon after illness, the dangers are many and not reserved for the unfit.

Simply stated, *you can die from running,* even when you're not a victim of hidden heart disease. The body, like any machine, can give out if the stress on it is too much at any given time. Your odds on collapse increase with age, certain physical and emotional characteristics (type A behavior, for example), and the amount of mileage piled on when conditions don't warrant it.

Death can come from too much, too soon — this is a theme that bears repeating. One of the more dangerous prescriptions came from the running community's own guru Dr. Kenneth Cooper. On page 53 of his very successful book *Aerobics,* written in 1968, Dr. Cooper describes a twelve-minute test to determine the fitness levels of anyone taking it.

The test is as follows: The person wishing to find his fitness level takes to a track or anywhere he can measure accurate distance. At a prearranged signal, he starts to run as fast as he can. The idea is simple: to run as far as one can in twelve minutes. That's it. All out for twelve minutes and a level of fitness can be evaluated.

Dr. Cooper's test has been quite popular. The problem — and a big one, at that — is that *you can die taking this twelve-minute test.* The strain of covering as much ground as possible in twelve minutes is tough enough on a fit athlete, but most of the people undergoing the test are beginners attempting to find out just how badly out of shape they are! Dr. Cooper's breakdown of fitness categories indicates that anything less than a mile and a quarter in twelve minutes is poor.[9]

The danger is taking this test when you're in poor physical condition. And the coincidental factor is that you're probably out of shape to be taking it in the first place. An experienced runner is not really interested in a fitness category, as he knows already what he can do under racing conditions. Therefore, a typical candidate for the test is usually a middle-aged, week-end runner taking to the local high school track, determined to show his friends and family that he can get into Cooper's top category by covering at least a mile and a half, or more, in twelve minutes. It's a real hazard.

Cooper sets the challenge clearly:

> Please keep in mind that it's a maximum test, and that it's your body being tested. I can't run behind you with a pitchfork to keep you going. You've got to push yourself very close to exhaustion. If the word "exhaustion" scares you, if you have any illness or clinical condition that requires treatment, or if you have any doubts about it all, definitely get your doctor's permission before taking the test.[10]

Is that enough of a warning for gung-ho week-end warriors? Probably not, since the challenge remains when Dr. Cooper takes a swipe at your ego with his *if* in the sentence about being scared by exhaustion. Most week-end athletes are not scared by exhaustion, they are not moved

136

by a mild disclaimer, and they are certainly not frightened of tackling the track and a twelve-minute death wish.

Yet two years after *Aerobics* captured the imagination of fitness buffs everywhere, Dr. Cooper had a change of heart. He decided that the twelve-minute test was not something to be taken so lightly. In his second book, *The New Aerobics,* he comments on the precautions necessary when taking the test:

> Don't take the fitness test prior to beginning an exercise program if you are over thirty years of age. Be sure to have a medical examination before you take a fitness test. If you are over thirty, it is still safer to postpone the test until you have completed the six-week "starter program." If you comply with the above, yet experience extreme fatigue, shortness of breath, light-headedness or nausea during the physical fitness test, stop immediately. Do not try to repeat the test until your fitness level has been gradually improved through regular exercise.[11]

What a change in approach! How different the language. The puzzling part of all this is that the first printing of *Aerobics* sold for at least a year before an updating was made at the time of paperback issue. How many people were injured or killed by the original advice to run until near exhaustion? We'll never know.

But Dr. Cooper is not the only one who promotes the

137

timed test without sufficient warning. Even *The Complete Runner,* one of the best-selling books from the editors of *Runner's World,* fails to mention the dangers involved with over stressing. This manual directs the individual interested in self-testing to run as far as possible in fifteen minutes, record that distance in meters; divide that by fifteen to determine speed in meters per minute; find maximum oxygen intake through this formula: (speed minus 133) X 1.72 + 33.3. A level of about 40, depending on age, is thought of as a minimum standard of fitness, but even less than dedicated joggers usually score higher than that.[12]

Where's the caveat in these instructions? Where's the warning about dropping dead if you're not prepared for an all-out 15-minute run? You won't find any warning. There are no problems mentioned.

I believe this is a highly dangerous and irresponsible attitude. Not only common sense but also the facts point out the dangers of all-out running when you're not sure of your conditioning. It can't be emphasized enough — you can drop dead from this kind of test.

Runner and author Hal Higdon wrote that it is easy to predict when a week-end athlete will die. He'll die on a weekend.[13] Let's expand that a bit and say that it's fairly easy to tell when a weekend will be fatal — when the week-end athlete is attempting the twelve- or fifteen-all-out running test.

Exercise-related deaths, especially when the exercise is running, should be carefully investigated. Although the potential dangers of strenuous exercise should not be overlooked, it would be unfair to claim that in *all* cases the activity alone had caused the fatality. There are a number of variables that have to be considered if the picture of sudden exercise death (SED) is to be complete.

First, running, or any type of exercise, is not the only key to maintaining fitness and good health. A person must have other areas of his life under control too. Stress in the home and/or workplace can add new dimensions to the word risk. Diet also applies. And competition figures into the picture, if we're to believe Rosenman and Friedman's type A behavior theory. In other words, running or any exercise in and by itself is not the one magic ingredient when it comes to overall fitness. All health factors, not just a single ideal, must be added together for a total picture of the person's state of being.

Second, some people have inherited a tendency toward heart attack. The risk is great and no amount of running will ever eliminate it. This type of person could very well expire in his sleep. However, the problems stemming from unbridled, uncontrolled running, without regard for the dangers involved, increase the danger for the heart attack-prone jogger.

Third, the type of running has much bearing on the risk of sudden heart failure. Anaerobic running, those short but very heavy bursts associated with middle-distance racing, can be more devastating than long, slow distance runs without the needless violence attached to sprinting.

Fourth, addiction to someone else's running program can spell disaster. The lure of marathoning, and now the added wonders of ultramarathoning (races above 26.2 miles), can mean taking part in races for which the individual is not prepared. A race of 50 or 100 miles, over all kinds of country and in all types of weather, is not the ideal for all runners. Nor is slavishly trying to follow another's training schedule, especially when the body rebels by sending out warning signals.

It has been estimated that about 8 per cent of America's men over the age of thirty-five have "silent" coronary disease, and that sudden death is quite common during activities that build up oxygen debt or raise the blood pressure significantly.[14] Running must be considered among these activities.

If you fervently desire death at an early mileage, follow the program outlined below:

Take up running in your middle thirties, especially if you're a male who is out of shape, overweight and used to sitting around the house. Make sure you don't have a complete physical examination (plus supervised stress test) first.

Take right off and run one of the popular twelve- to fifteen-minute tests popularized by the running gurus. Show the kids you can still reach into yesteryear and hit those quarter miles much as you think you did years ago, in high school.

If you survive the test, and you probably will, begin to run far and fast, right away. Begin thinking of the local marathon since it's fast approaching.

Ignore aches, pains and little illnesses that seem to plague you from the beginning. After all, pain is an indication that you're finally getting somewhere in this exercise game!

And finally, and probably most important to your suicide by inches, compare yourself to the really class runners who are all over the pages of the running magazines. After all, just because some of these runners have youth, years of training, and some natural talent, doesn't mean *you* can't make haste toward some personal records.

If this plan seems cynical, it's meant to be just that. If you look at the foolhardy suggestions I've made, however, you'll see that they aren't too far off what we've been looking at all through this book. People do take up running after years of inactivity, and with little or no preparation, and no medical checkup. People do take those twelve-

and fifteen-minute tests to find out how much endurance they don't have. People do run ignoring physical problems. And people do compare themselves to champions and ignore the preparation and natural ability of these runners. If that weren't the case, most of the magazines filled with biographical information (including what the champions eat for breakfast and what color socks they prefer on warm days) wouldn't sell so well. People want to know that if they eat spaghetti before the big race it'll give them endurance over the long haul. After all, Joe Runner, six-time marathon champion, does it all the time, and you can see him actually eating the pasta on page 50 of the latest magazine.

We're all going to die sooner or later. That's a fact. Only we all prefer to make it much later. Most of us feel guilty about our increasingly sedentary lives. We are constantly reminded that we eat too much, work too hard while enjoying it less, spend too much time in front of the television set, and ignore the natural rejuvenation of physical play. In short, we're told that we have turned into a nation of slobs. And that hurts.

At the same time, however, we're subtly (and not so subtly) told by the running subculture (and all those who make money off running) that exercise, especially running, will renew our shattered lives and push the dreaded specter of death into the shadows. We'll have a kind of eternal youth. All it will take is some running today, more tomorrow, and so on. Running, running and more running will do it all. We can not only tell ourselves we're doing right, but all of the tee-shirts patches, certificates and running shoes are visual reminders that the promise must be true.

But in reality the dangers exist. We know that now. People are being injured. Some are even dying. It is imperative that we treat running with the respect it is due, if more casualties are to be avoided. We must look beyond the attractive promises, the slick packaging and the persuasive gurus. We must be as aware of the dark side of running as we are mesmerized by its bright side.

NOTES FROM CHAPTER SIX

1. Lawrence Meyer, "Marathoner's Death Sends Tremor Through Runner's World," *Portland Oregonian,* 13 October 1978.

2. *Runner's World,* September 1978, p. 18.

3. Hal Higdon, *Fitness After Forty* (Mountain View, California: World Publications, 1977), pp. 102-121.

4. Ibid.

5. Ibid.

6. Irving M. Levetos with Libby Machal, *You Can Beat The Odds on a Heart Attack* (New York: Bobbs-Merrill, 1975), p. 244.

7. William Fossbender, *You and Your Health* (New York: Wiley, 1977), p. 244.

8. Meyer Friedman and Ray H. Rosenman, *Type A Behavior and Your Heart* (New York: Alfred A. Knopf, 1974), p. 158.

9. Kenneth H. Cooper, *Aerobics* (New York: M. Evans and Company, Inc., 1968), p. 54.

10. Ibid., p. 53.

11. Kenneth H. Cooper, *The New Aerobics* (New York: M. Evans and Company, Inc., 1970), p. 29.

12. *Runner's World, Complete Runner,* p. 75.

13. Higdon, *Fitness After Forty,* p. 197.

14. Sheehan, *Encyclopedia of Athletic Medicine,* p. 70.

CHAPTER SEVEN: DEMYSTIFYING CVE (CARDIOVASCULAR ENDURANCE): A LEXICON

"The first adaptation to dehydration is to raise the body temperature. By this, the temperature gradient between the body center and the skin surface is increased so that the transfer of heat to the skin surface is facilitated without requiring a diversion of blood from the muscles."

Joe Henderson, ed.
The Complete Marathoner

Activity Drunkard: A term coined in the 1960s to mean anyone overtrained, overactive, overanxious and over-developed. This pejorative term can be applied to some marathon runners.

Aerobic: Any exercise that uses oxygen in large amounts

over an extended period. Therefore, even slow running is an aerobic exercise, even if the pace is comfortable.

Aerobics: An exercise program developed by Dr. Kenneth H. Cooper of Dallas, Texas, that employs activities using oxygen in large amounts. Such activities include running, swimming (as long as it's not floating around on an air mattress), and cycling. Advocates of aerobics claim that consistent exercise of this kind will build real fitness; e.g., cardiovascular fitness.

Anaerobic: Any strenuous exercise of short but heavy duration that leaves the exerciser breathless. An example of an anaerobic activity is climbing stairs. Some experts feel that extended periods of anaerobic exercise can be dangerous as the body can't cope with the strain.

Arrhythmia: Any variation from the normal heart rhythm. Running deaths from heat prostration can usually be attributed to severe arrhythmia.

Ascorbic Acid: Complicated talk for vitamin C. According to some pundits, large amounts can help alleviate some of the effects from too much running.

Automobile: A major danger to runners who attempt to challenge it on the street.

Blood Pressure: The pressure of the blood within the vessels. Elevated pressure above the norm is known as *hypertension* and can be extremely hazardous to health. Most runners feel that exercising keeps blood pressure

146

within normal limits.

Body Type: Classifying human beings according to their size and shape. Ectomorphs and mesomorphs are examples. Such classification is sometimes known as *somatyping.*

Bromhydrosis: Excessive sweating of the feet accompanied by a bad odor.

Bursitis: Inflammation of a saclike body cavity (especially one located between joints). A very painful condition sometimes known as "tennis elbow" or "pitcher's arm." This condition is also common among runners and can be debilitating if not treated.

Calories: A heat unit used to measure the energy requirements of the body and energy supplied by various foods. Also, a unit of measure everyone counts *after* finishing off a large meal!

Carbohydrate Loading: The eating of starches before a marathon on the theory that the body will more readily use the carbohydrates as fuel. (A plot by spaghetti manufacturers to increase the popularity of pasta?)

Cardiovascular Endurance (CVE): The efficiency of the heart and circulatory system (including the use of oxygen). The major reason most runners prefer their brand of exercise over any other.

Chondromalacia: A stress injury of the knee; one of the most common injuries in running and affecting more than

147

half of the joggers who complain of being hurt. Usually known as "runner's knee."

Counter: The cup forming the back of a running shoe, supporting the heel laterally and protecting vertically. A poor counter will lead the unsuspecting runner to an injury-ridden experience. Insufficient heel counters are most commonly found on inexpensive shoes that have stripes, swooshes and color-coordinated design — but no protection for the user.

Dehydration: The loss of body fluids to the point of danger; a condition easily attained by runners in warm, humid weather.

Desirable Weight: The weight in relation to body height and age that is considered optimum by actuarial experience.

Dog: A territorially jealous creature that can make things difficult for any runner breaching the unseen, unknown zone. An animal that can outrun a man because he has twice as many legs.

Dyspnea: Difficulty in getting one's breath. This condition in running usually signals danger and an immediate cutback in activity. It can be associated with anaerobic exercise.

Ectomorph: A body type usually described as lean and lanky; most noticeable at the starting line of any distance race (where everyone else looks like an ectomorph!).

Ectopic Heartbeat: Skipped beats; sometimes noticed in highly developed runners due to the strengthening of the heart muscle and an improved electrical impulse within the heart itself.

Edema: Swelling caused by accumulation of fluid in the tissues. It can occur in the feet of a runner who is over-stressing.

Endurance: The reserves within a body that can be called upon to withstand physical hardship.

Fad: A briefly popular fashion. Running seems to have the longevity to be considered more than a current fad.

Fartlek: A Swedish term for "speed play." This is a form of nontrack (woods, fields, roads, etc.) running and sprinting with the pace dictated by the conditions of the environment and the runner. Sometimes known as "roving," "cruising," or "wogging" as it involves various paces and no set plan.

Fasting: The absence of food for periods of time (usually no less than twenty-four hours). Can (with a physician's approval) be beneficial to runners as well as nonrunners.

Fitness: A possible synonym for health, but a more narrow term applied mostly to the exercise phenomenon.

Fun-Running: Informal running not geared for competition. Some people would say that no form of running can ever be labeled *fun.*

Glue Gun: A special piece of equipment for melting a rubber compound onto running shoes that are worn at the tread. If correctly done (so that the thicknesses of heels and soles of both shoes are the same), such repairs can extend the life of the shoes and help keep expenses down.

Glycogen: A substance the body makes from carbohydrates; used as energy and stored in the livers of most animals.

Gun Lap: The final lap of any race on a track (above one-quarter mile or one lap itself). A signal to the competitors that the race will end with the lap they're starting.

Health: Stated as the optimal functioning of the organism and freedom from disease. Sometimes health is synonymous with fitness when viewed by the running community.

Heat Exhaustion: State of shock characterized by weak pulse, shallow breathing, increased sweating and a cool, moist skin. Nausea, vomiting and dizziness also occur, as can fainting.

Heat Stroke: State of overexposure to sun and heat; characterized by dizziness, a slowing of the pulse, increased body temperature and dryness of the mouth and skin. Convulsions can occur. Unconsciousness may result. *Death can occur from heat stroke.*

Holistic Training: An exercise program that measures the parts against the whole and considers everything that may be important to the exerciser. Holistic training looks at the relationship of muscular strength to cardiac efficiency, and so on.

Hyperthermia: Higher than normal temperature of the body, sometimes caused by overexposure to heat and sun. A definite threat to a runner who is not properly prepared.

Hypothermia: Subnormal temperature of the body, sometimes caused by overexposure to cold, wind, and dampness. A *definite danger to an unsuspecting runner.*

Iliopsoas: Muscles in the front of the thigh that can become too tight from overuse; can trigger back problems.

Intervals: Alternating fast and slow runs with periods of walking and jogging. This form of intense training can *lead to injury* from overuse and stressing.

Jogamute: Getting to and from your job on foot; obviously coined during this era of fuel shortages and encouraged by government in an attempt to reduce the use of automobiles.

Jogging: A synonym for running. Some runners and authors differentiate between jogging and running based on the pace being set. For example, some writers believe that any pace slower than eight minutes per mile is jogging, faster than eight minutes per mile is running. Jogging is praised by the running community, praised by some of the medical profession, and damned by individuals, including philosopher Alan Watts who treats jogging contemptuously in his autobiography *(In My Own Way,* New York: Random House, 1973) as "a style of flat-footed running which jolts the bones, jangles the nerves, and is supposed to turn you into a real man."

Jogtrot: A variation of jogwalk.

Jogwalk: Very slow running that nearly resembles a fast walk.

Juniors: A racing class — all runners aged nineteen and under.

Kick: The finishing sprint at the end of a race. Usually your condition after competing over a distance can be easily seen by the kick.

Kilometer: An international form of measurement; approximately 5/8 of a mile (3280.8 feet per kilometer as compared to 5280 feet per mile).

Kinesiology: The study of human movement.

Knee: The joint between the upper and lower parts of the human leg. The section of the anatomy most injured by runners due to overstressing.

Longevity: Long duration of life. One of the specific benefits of cardiovascular exercise that is sometimes promised by the running subculture. This hypothesis remains to be proven.

Long Sprints: 1/8 mile to 1/2 mile. A very hazardous distance for the unconditioned athlete. This distance can usually mean anaerobic exercise and a strain on the body.

Long Distance Running: Any distance above six miles.

LSD: An acronym for long slow distance, a concept put forth by some runners that holds for slow mileage as a training exercise. The concept includes the idea that the long slow distance will create a training effect important to cardiovascular fitness *without* placing a strain on the muscles and tendons. Adherents of LSD feel that injuries are less with this system.

Masters: An age-group class: forty years and over for men, and thirty years and over for women. A category that has allowed many older runners to compete in races which might formerly have been restricted to younger runners.

Marathon: Historically, any endurance contest that takes a fairly long period of time to complete; e.g., marathon dancing in the 1930s. However, lately it has become identified with a foot race that is 26 miles, 385 yards, 11 inches in length. World-class runners can cover this distance in a little over two hours. There's no official world record though since no two courses are alike.

Mesomorph: Muscular body type.

Middle-Distance Running: 1/2 to 6 miles.

Morton's Foot: A short first toe combined with a long second toe. This mechanical defect, more common than first suspected, can create problems for the jogger. Morton's Toe will affect many parts of the body, due to the closed system (one part of the body creating stress in another part of the anatomy).

Motivation: Synonym for will power, a characteristic of all exercise programs. The lack of motivation will usually cut a program short no matter how ambitious the commitment.

Muggers: A serious danger to the runner, especially in urban settings.

Necrosis: Tissue death in relatively small, localized areas. Sometimes heart tissue dies, leaving the runner vulnerable to more serious consequences.

Neuritis: Inflammation of a nerve causing pain, loss of reflexes, and sometimes muscular atrophy. A *real danger* to runners from overuse.

Nutrition: The overall processes of growth, repair and maintenance of an organism. The relation of nutrition to exercise is a subject of debate both in and out of the running community. Some running buffs believe nutrition must be as carefully planned as their running schedules, while others eat almost anything that tastes good and stays down.

Obesity: Extreme weight; a concept rarely thought about by runners.

Orthotics: A foot support to help maintain the foot in a functionally neutral position. Many times this device is the difference between pain-free jogging and no running at all.

Overstriding: The taking of extralarge steps in running. Sometimes overstriding can lead to injury if the runner is striding beyond a comfortable distance.

Overuse: In exercise, the concept of doing too much. It can lead to injuries or illness, or both.

Pace: The average rate of running.

Physical Fitness: Sometimes used synonymously for health. It is the optimum organic operation of the organism.

Podiatrist: A doctor specializing in the treatment of feet; one who has come into his own during the running boom.

P. R.: Short for "personal record." A running term for a time or distance never before achieved by that particular runner. (This allows mediocrity to become a record-breaker).

Race Walking: Competitive walking at a pace that can be as grueling as any running event.

Racing: Competitive running and the time when injuries are most prevalent.

Recovery: The amount of time required to rebuild energy

levels after a difficult effort. Sometimes this is measured by the time it takes for the pulse to return to its resting rate.

Running: A term covering all paces above a walk or beyond a jog, depending on where you're coming from in the argument between runners and joggers.

Running Addiction: The dependency on regular cardio-vascular exercise in the form of running that can lead to withdrawal symptoms when the exercise is stopped for a period of time.

Rupture: A tear in a soft tissue; e.g., tendon rupture.

Sciatica: Inflammation of the sciatic nerve from the lower back to the toe. It can be a very painful condition and can sideline a runner.

Secondary Amenorrhea: A cessation of normal menstruation. A problem that can affect female runners who have lost large amounts of weight from their heavy exercise program.

Senior: A term interchangeable with Masters.

Shin Splints: Pain and tenderness along the shin bone; a common running problem.

Short Sprints: Any distance under 1/8 of a mile.

Specificity: Exercise improvements made in training that are *specific* to the *type* of training involved; e.g., weight lifting is specific to the muscles that are worked on; running is specific to other areas not always touched by the weights.

Stitch: A sharp pain in the side of a runner that can be created by faulty breathing or food in the stomach. Some runners are more prone to stitches than others.

Stress: The total of all energy demands on the body, both mental and physical.

Sudden Exercise Death (SED): The death of an exerciser during training or competitive event.

Surmanage: An Italian term for overtraining, or a staleness brought on by too much exercise.

Tendinitis: Inflammation of the tendon. This can be serious and is prevalent, in different forms, among many runners.

Territorial Imperative: A dog's territory that a runner can accidentally invade. This invasion usually invites attack from the animal.

Third Wind: An alleged "high" that comes about thirty minutes into a running workout.

Training Effect: Fitness improvement from regular exercise; sometimes can even take place a day or two after the exercise program.

Type A Behavior: A set of personality characteristics that may contribute to an increased risk of coronary artery and heart disease.

Type B Behavior: A set of personality characteristics that may *not* contribute to the increased risk of coronary artery and heart disease.

Ultradistance: A synonym for an ultramarathon.

Ultramarathon: Any distance above 26.3 miles.

Valgus: An outward rolling of the feet.

Varus: An inward rolling of the feet.

Ventricular Fibrillation: An irregular heartbeat that can quickly *lead to death* if not treated.

Virus: A pathological agent of infection; something a runner should not take lightly.

Walking: A gait whereby the feet are raised and lowered in alternate fashion. A fine exercise that can bring about cardiovascular fitness with a minimum of injuries.

Wall: The hypothetical point in a distance race where a runner is suddenly and overwhelmingly exhausted. In the marathon this comes about at the twenty-mile mark. Some runners swear they have "hit the wall," while others feel there is no such inhibiting point.

Warmdown: A postexercise set of stretching moves

158

to bring the body from stress to rest. A very important part of any runner's schedule. Also usually ignored.

Warmup: A preexercise set of stretching moves to prepare the body for stress. A very important part of any runner's schedule, but unfortunately usually ignored.

Wogging: A combination of walking and jogging.

Yogaerobics: A set of yoga stretching exercises that are alleged to provide a good accompaniment to cardiovascular exercise.

Zen of Running: The more mystical side of running, aimed at new highs from cardiovascular exercise. Adherents see it as a "head" trip.

CHAPTER EIGHT:
DEMYSTIFICATION CONTINUED:
AN ANNOTATED BIBLIOGRAPHY

"The problem that faces the newcomer
to the field is the great array of books
all with promising titles, all with
intriguing authors."

Robert E. Burger
Jogger's Catalog: The Source Book for Runners

The books that follow have been carefully selected and examined from the point of view we've been exploring all along: that running must be treated seriously and with the utmost caution, and that running *may not be for everyone* who decides to lace on a pair of running shoes and hit the streets.

161

This bibliography will enable the reader to choose from the hundreds of books and magazines available. Running books, by and large fall into one of three categories (with some overlap). The first category is that of the general "how-to" book. This gives the reader tips, training schedules, equipment hints, and generally provides all the positive material a runner might need to understand his exercise commitment. But notice — I said *positive* material. Most of these how-to books relegate the negative aspects of running to the back of the book and try not to discourage the neophyte.

The second category is that of the morale-builder book. This is usually written by a famous runner who delights in telling stories and anecdotes about his running career. This type of book makes for interesting reading and sometimes passes on information on injuries that are associated with running. The morale-builder book is inspirational and fun to peruse.

The third category, newer than the other two and growing by the issue, is that of the "head-trip" books. This type of book represents the Zen influence on running and usually maintains somewhere within the pages that running will bring about new highs. These books are enjoyable and a little on the preposterous side.

The selected bibliography that follows should be read

as carefully as everything else that has come before it. (This is not just my way of showing you how many books I read to prepare myself for this one.)

One final note: Read *selectively* and *carefully*. There are just too many opinions to try and follow them all!

Ald, Roy. *Jogging, Aerobics and Diet.* New York: New American Library, 1973.

One of the first books on the market stressing the interrelation of the three most important elements of physical fitness; exercise, oxygen and diet. This is probably one of the better books since the author doesn't make too many claims about running that can lead the neophyte into trouble. However, the book doesn't list the dangers that do exist. It was written by an enthusiastic runner who really understands his field and some of the expressions used are encouraging to the new runner. For example, on page 19 you'll find a three-part axiom that says bluntly: "Get that oxygen! Pass the oxygen around inside! Use the oxygen to burn up the food for energy!" The book also contains training schedules and recipes for health foods.

163

Anderson, Bob, and Henderson, Joe, eds. *Guide to Distance Running*. Mountain View, California: World Publications, 1971.

Another early book, the beginning of a long line from World Publications (*Runner's World* magazine). Many pictures and a kind of overview of the running game. Not too many negative aspects are outlined because this book came out early in the accelerating growth of running. It is definitely dated.

Anderson, James, and Cohen, Martin. *The West Point Fitness and Diet Book*. New York: Rawson Associates, 1977.

An excellent all-around book stressing stretching and weights, as well as cardiovascular exercise. Injuries are covered lightly in the back of the book. Chapter 12 (Tips on Better Performance) discusses some of the problems associated with exercise and with running itself. This is really *not* one of the standard running books touted by the running community.

Bannister, Roger. *The Four Minute Mile*. New York: Dodd, Mead, 1955.

One of those very rare books about the pain of running and the price of excellence. Dr. Roger Bannister, first man to run the mile in less than four minutes (3 minutes

59.4 seconds in 1954), expresses clearly the difficulty in preparing for such an undertaking. He also provides insight into the individuality of training and why the recipe for running must meet the requirements of each person. This book may be difficult to find.

Batten, Jack. *The Complete Jogger.* New York: Harcourt Brace Jovanovich, 1977.

One of a litany of books that are "complete" in all aspects of running. Author Batten is so in love with running that it is difficult for him to say much that isn't absolutely exuberant about his chosen exercise. He does, however, scare the hell out of the reader on page 87, by quoting Canadian distance runner Bruce Kidd: "There are moments of such torture and helplessness that you'd turn your mother in to the Gestapo if only they'd allow you to stop." He also writes about hammer toes, blood in the urine and cramps in the liver, a byproduct of a sugar deficiency in the blood called hypoglycemia which is *common among marathoners.* (Emphasis mine.)

Batten gives some antirunning doctors a turn too, quoting Dr. Joseph Beninson of Detroit's Henry Ford Hospital, "Jogging squashes your spine like an accordion;" Dr. Don Lannin, physician to the Minesota Vikings, "Jogging has too much bang-bang and that is particularly damaging to the hip;" and the infamous Dr. J.E. Schmidt

165

who infuriated the running community with his out-
rageous attack on jogging in a popular men's magazine,
"Among the casualties of jogging are the dropped
stomach, the loose spleen, the floating kidney and the
fallen arches."

One of the more interesting books for the beginner
and one that will help him become excited about his
newly chosen form of cardiovascular exercise.

Benyo, Richard. *Return to Running.* Mountain View, California: World Publications, 1978.

A morale-builder book by a runner of the World Publications stable. Interesting to read about the comeback.
This type of book mixes the funny with the sad and the
poignant with the silly. Author Benyo tells his readers of
all the trials and tribulations connected with trying to
return from the running of his youth to the running of
his post youth (or whatever comes before the stigma
of middle-age).

Benyo, Richard, ed. *The Complete Woman Runner.* Mountain View, California: World Publications, 1978.

The title says it all. A large book with a large price;
however, much like other books by *Runner's World*
editors (for example, *The Complete Runner* and *The
Complete Marathoner*) this release tends to cover all

aspects of running for the umpteenth time. The fact that it is supposed to be aimed at the women in the running audience is only coincidental. Very few of the concepts involved are for women only. A readable book.

Bowerman, William J., and Harris, W. E. *Jogging: A Complete Physical Fitness Program for All Ages.* New York: Grosset & Dunlap, 1967.

The seminal thoughts on jogging that last and last and last. Bill Bowerman, coach at the University of Oregon, one of the running schools in this country, constructs a sane, sensible plan for starting out in the very strenuous cardiovascular area. He was the first to recommend that people "train and not strain," and he had some practical advice that remains important years later, to wit, if you can't talk while running, you're probably running too fast. Now that running has become quasi-scientific in the latest books, Bowerman's simple directive becomes more involved (such as measuring pulse rates against maximal rates, etc.). One of the best books for a beginner and still a bargain in the bookstores where many running books have escalated in price.

Burger, Robert E. *Jogger's Catalog: The Source Book for Runners.* New York: M. Evans & Company, 1978.

A delightful compendium of products, books, ideas, and

lots more for the running fan. In a world where collections of this and that are extremely popular, author Burger has brought together the kinds of information that enable the reader to choose the right paraphernalia for him. Again, the author is in love with jogging and treats it in the most positive manner possible. *Jogger's Catalog* is fun reading (witness part of a quote – just one of hundreds of clever quotes in the book – from Erich Segal: "It is a scientific fact that running is, by chance, salubrious as well. But so is sex. Yet has a man in passion ever cried, "I only do it for my health?") There are book reviews in this catalog and lots of pictures. Probably the best all-around introduction to the running phenomenon that can be picked up in your local bookstore.

Cooper, Kenneth H. *Aerobics.* New York: M. Evans & Co., 1968.

One of the first books touting aerobics conditioning and the concept that running is about the best form of cardiovascular fitness around. The dangerous twelve-minute test exists in the original hardbound version and must be looked at with a jaundiced eye. Dr. Cooper's enthusiasm for his program should be measured against the complexity of keeping a point system for daily workouts, and the creeping boredom that can enter into the commitment.

168

Cooper, Kenneth H. *The New Aerobics.* New York: M. Evans & Co., 1970.

An updating of his first book with additional point charts for various types of exercises. The twelve-minute test appears with a lengthy and quite vocal disclaimer about taking it without a medical clearance.

Cooper, Kenneth H. *The Aerobics Way: New Data on the World's Most Popular Exercise Program* New York: M. Evans & Co., 1977.

Additional charts, more interesting revelations on the exercise phenomenon, and lengthy descriptions of Dr. Cooper's new facilities in Dallas, Texas. This is the most complex of his books on the aerobics concept and can give the beginning runner a feeling that there's more to conditioning than meets the eye. And so there is!

Cooper, Mildred, and Cooper, Kenneth H. *Aerobics for Women.* New York: M. Evans & Co., 1972.

The first book introducing women to the wonders of cardiovascular conditioning. This book by the Coopers helped make running respectable for thousands of women all over America. Some of the claims, however, can't be substantiated and only add to the idea that running is the only exercise there is. For example, on page 30, the authors claim to have evidence that running increases fertility. Not so. The problems with the possible disruption of a woman's menses indicate that this could actually be the opposite.

Consumer's Guide editors. *The Running Book.* New York: Crown Publishers, 1978.

A collection of the tips, hints and recipes that are the staple of most running books. This one is well put together and fairly simple. One of the best features is the price. The book, however, falls into the same trap as most running books: few of the hazards are pointed out to be as serious as they really are.

Daniels, Jack; Fitts, Robert; and Sheehan, George. *Conditioning for Distance Running.* New York: John Wiley & Sons, 1978.

A complex book written for the serious athlete and/or his coach. After reading this effort you'll realize that some of the ideas behind conditioning are not as simple as described by other authors. The warp and the woof of conditioning require taking into account many variables, some of them on a scientific basis. Interesting book to peruse.

Diporta, Leo. *Zen Running.* New York: Everest House, 1978.

A definite head-trip book. One of many that attempts to mesmerize the runner into believing that his chosen exercise will lift him into a state of euphoria. Some joggers do claim exceptional benefits from running; however, this has yet to be proved on a wide basis. Interesting, but without the dangers spelled out.

Emmerton, Bill. *The Official Book of Running.* New York: Bookcraft Guild, 1978.

Bill Emmerton is the runner's runner when it comes to traversing huge distances under less than ideal conditions. He has run across continents, searing deserts and over mountain ranges. Not exactly your average jogger. The book is filled with personal tips on the running "game." His earlier book (*Running for Your Life,* New York: World Publishing Co., 1970) touched upon the basic weaknesses of modern life with a very eloquent description of Joe Slob, his sweets-filled breakfast, sedentary job, alcohol-befogged lunch, and subsequent coronary. Interesting writing by a man who seems to defy ordinary dangers by treating running as a mania.

Falls, Joe. *The Boston Marathon.* New York: Macmillan, 1977.

Reporter Falls brings the greatest of marathons alive in this book. If you are wondering what it's like to run at Boston (or any of the larger marathons), this book is surely worth the price of purchase. Many of the severe problems associated with covering 26.3 miles are spelled out. It seems well balanced and not just another glowing report from Framingham, Massachusetts. There is also an excellent chapter on Clarence DeMar, seven-time winner of the race and the man with the incredible cardiovascular system.

Fanning, Tony, and Fanning, Robbie. *Keep Running.* New York: Simon & Schuster, 1978.

In the genre of how-to books, spiced here and there with morale builders. This husband-and-wife team encourages runners to hit the streets and start the clean life! Interesting, but just another book on running.

Fixx, James F. *The Complete Book of Running.* New York: Random House, 1977.

The grandest and most popular book ever on running. Author Fixx seems to have something to say about every aspect of running in this attractive tome (including a cover that is hypnotic and probably one reason for the high sales). You'll find that injuries are played down and that the hazards are well balanced off by all of the positive attributes Mr. Fixx finds in running. He is definitely in love with his exercise and is not in the least ashamed to try and proselytize the reader.

There are an abundance of drawings and charts that really don't add too much to the text. Sometimes Mr. Fixx gets taken in by an anecdote that turns out to be one of the popular jokes of running. For example, on page 49 we find the following (probably the most repeated story in running literature): "an incidental cold-weather hazard — though not, I am happy to say, a common one if you dress properly — was described not long ago in the New England Journal of Medicine by Dr. Melvin Hershkowitz of Jersey City, New Jersey. It is frostbite of the penis, and it was incurred by a fifty-three-year-old physician during a thirty-minute run in below-freezing weather. Fortunately, symptoms disappeared within a few minutes. The patient, according to the report, has instituted rigorous precautionary measures." Great story — but only a joke by Dr. Hershkowitz.

I asked Jim Fixx if he wasn't taking this frostbite of the penis too seriously. He responded to me by saying, "I thought I was treating that penis business as a joke."

173

You can decide for yourself.

This is probably the only how-to book you'll ever need as a beginner, but beware of the author's love affair with running. Just as all love affairs are blind, this book lacks some of the caveats required for safe and sane exercising.

Friedman, Meyer, and Rosenman, Ray H. *Type A Behavior and Your Heart*. New York: Alfred A. Knopf, 1974.

This may seem like a strange book to be included with all of the running books. It's certainly not a how-to book on running, it's definitely not a morale builder, and it certainly can't qualify as a head-trip book. What this book is, however, is the first severe criticism of running by the medical community. The two cardiologists would never qualify as friends of the running community, but their book certainly must be taken seriously. Their criticism levels jogging for the moment and has to be looked at straight on, rather than dismissing it with a wave of the running shoe on the grounds that old men such as Rosenman and Friedman are against anything physical because they aren't involved with it on a personal level. This is like saying that any criticism of football can only come from participants, or that a doctor who speaks out against the growing problem with drugs should not be listened to unless he's taking those drugs himself. This is narrow thinking, indeed.

Rosenman and Friedman have points that *must be considered.* Their book has to be read along with the more glowing books on running.

Geline, Robert J. *The Practical Runner.* New York: Collier Books, 1978.

Add this to the proliferation of how-to books. This one offers the usual variety of tips, hints and recipes for successful running. Dangers — not too many indicated here. Author Geline is in love with his exercise.

Gilmore, Haydn. *Jog For Your Life.* Grand Rapids, Michigan: Zondervan Publishing House, 1974.

Mr. Gilmore's book is a head-trip with religious overtones. Filled with many pictures of people running over beautiful hills and down bucolic roads, some of the book's ideas seem more personal than general. One of the first books to treat running as more than a physical exercise.

Glasser, William. *Positive Addiction.* New York: Harper & Row, 1976.

Dr. Glasser advances the unique idea that participating

in a positive, repetitive sport or recreation that can be done fairly well is a great reinforcement for mental well-being. Running fills this spot. An interesting approach and well within the head-trip category. Since *Positive Addiction,* Dr. Glasser has been a favorite of the running community.

Glover, Bob, and Shepherd, Jack. *The Runner's Handbook: A Complete Fitness Guide for Men and Women on the Run.* New York: Penguin Books, 1978.

The word "complete" in the title gives this away as another of the how-to books bent on turning every man, woman and child into a gentle jogger. The authors are generous with their tips, hints and training schedules but, alas, the dangers are played down and driven to the rear of the book. It is difficult to imagine that too many more "complete" running books are ahead of us, but apparently they sell, and sell very well.

Henderson, Joe. *Long Slow Distance: The Humane Way to Train.* Mountain View, California: World Publications, 1970.

If you look at the copyright date you'll see that this one breaks fertile ground. Joe Henderson's book is the first attempt at producing a safe running program by stressing slow jogging. A very readable book by an interesting author. The first of many books by Mr. Henderson.

Henderson, Joe. *Run Gently, Run Long.* Mountain View, California: World Publications, 1974.

A typical Henderson book with tips and ideas for the new runner as well as the experienced jogger. This book continues to promote the concept of long slow distance over the more feverish aerobics of Ken Cooper. A good book for your personal library.

Henderson, Joe. *The Long-Run Solution.* Mountain View, California: World Publications, 1976.

Hendersonian in concept, Hendersonian in production; additional anecdotes and ideas on his favorite exercise. This is one more in the continuing saga of Henderson's love of running.

Henderson, Joe. *Jog, Run, Race.* Mountain View, California: World Publications, 1977.

Another in the series of Henderson books. This effort offers training, schedules, a dictionary of running terms and just about everything needed to move from gentle jogging to hard running to the world of competitive racing. A good book.

Henderson, Joe, ed. *The Complete Marathoner.* Mountain View, California: World Publications, 1978.

The title gives it away. This is the book that contains all of the ingredients needed to move into the heady atmosphere of marathoning. The chapters cover everything from the lure of the run to moving up to ultra-distance running. Schedules and training tips from the best marathoners in the world are included. However, the dangers seem to be surrounded by so much positive reinforcement that it is difficult not to become enamored with the marathon race at the cost of ignoring the hazards. There's really little to add about marathoning that isn't in this compendium of running lore.

Henning, Joel. *Holistic Running: Beyond the Threshold of Fitness.* New York: New American Library, 1978.

A head-trip book that provides more Zen-type information about jogging. The author pushes the idea that running is a kind of meditative recreation that can do much for the spirit. Interesting reading, but does not address the problems that exist with the physical side of cardiovascular exercise.

Higdon, Hal. *On the Run From Dogs and People.* Chicago: Henry Regnery, 1971.

An amusing morale-builder book by a really fine writer.

Hal Higdon provides anecdotes on the more mundane aspects of trying to cope with jogging around the local streets and parks. Worth reading.

Higdon, Hal. *Beginning Runner's Guide.* Mountain View, California: World Publications, 1978.

Another compendium of information for the neophyte; it seems that "guide" competes with "complete" for the newly addicted runner's attention. Higdon is one of the better writers on this subject and his book gives training tips to the newcomer. Hazards — again played down.

Higdon, Hal. *Fitness After Forty.* Mountain View, California: World Publications, 1977.

One of the best and entirely underrated in the area of running books. Higdon has the courage to tell us about the unexplained running deaths. His chapter on these deaths can't be matched anywhere.

He can be absolutely charming (the amusing longevity test at the end of the book), or quite profound (the detailed report on fitness testing around this country). One of the best overall books on running. Maybe what it needs are the magic words — the book should be called *The Complete Fitness After Forty Book,* or *A Complete Guide to Fitness After Forty.*

Any way you look at this book, it's a winner.

Hlavac, Harry. *The Foot Book: Advice for Athletes* Mountain View, California: World Publications, 1977.

Once the running subculture was forced to admit that injuries *do* occur with alarming frequency, it was just a matter of time before a book arrived on the scene describing in detail how the human foot is constructed, how it is injured, and what to do to prevent these debilitating injuries.

There are serious discussions on equipment, running surfaces, and congenital defects that produce injuries in runners who seemingly take care of themselves. An expensive book, but well worth the price to have it on hand to prevent your own misery.

Kavanagh, Terence. *Heart Attack? Counterattack.* New York: Van Nostrand Reinhold, 1976.

An interesting account of how heart attack patients who had been condemned to inaction were able to return to fit and healthy lives. Some of the Kavanagh coronary victims entered and finished the Boston Marathon. Part of the book is technical; however it is interesting reading and lays out carefully the plan for replacing sedentary living with a running program. This is not your usual running book.

Kiell, Paul J., and Frelinghuysen, Joseph S. *Keep Your Heart Running*. New York: Winchester Press, 1976.

This has been re-released as *The Complete Guide to Physical Fitness*. Another how-to book much like the *West Point Fitness and Diet Book*, it offers a potpourri of information on exercise, weights, running, diet, and so on.

It seems that the book suffers from two different writing styles though; for example, sometimes the writing is clear and easy to understand but sometimes it is diffuse and very technical. The dangers of running are spelled out in part, but as in the case of fluid loss, in a difficult style to read. In the chapter titled "Fluid and Electrolyte Management in High-Stress Physical Exercise," the authors say in part: "The acute dehydration that accompanies profuse sweating while running in the heat causes a reduction in extracellular fluid and a significant lowering of the runner's blood volume" (p. 201).

An interesting book from two enthusiastic runners.

Knuttgen, Howard G., and Shepro, David. *Complete Conditioning: The No-Nonsense Guide to Fitness and Good Health*. Reading, Massachusetts: Addison-Wesley Publishing Co., 1975.

If you look closely at the title you'll see that it contains many of the magic elements that create a successful running book: "complete," "guide," "fitness," and the popular term "health."

Seriously, this book has some very interesting pointers on getting in shape, but the authors use tongue-in-cheek approaches to some of their information. For example, on page 146, amidst a lexicon, we find "Gardening for Fitness." The authors tell us that "as a CV conditioning activity, gardening is located somewhere lower than golf." Really? "Fishing for Fitness" on the same page brings the definition of "Just that!" Really?

The book is really better than these two examples, though. Again, one of the older books and not overly concerned with injuries from running.

Kostrubala, Thaddeus. *The Joy of Running.* J. B. Lippincott Co., 1976.

A very successful approach to running by a San Diego psychiatrist. He claims that some of his emotionally upset patients have been brought back to a more stable condition by a running program. The positive side of running, therefore, is stressed to the point of excluding the dangers we must face. Worth your time to read this one.

Kuntzleman, Charles T., ed. *The Physical Fitness Encyclopedia.* Emmaus, Pennsylvania: Rodale Books, 1970.

Probably hard to find at this point; however, a book filled with definitions, descriptions and pictures that underline the various ideas of exercise. Some of the earliest aerobic information is in this book as well as some items not found anywhere else (including the amusing "activity drunkard" definition on page 1). This is the kind of book to have on your library shelf along with the newer books on individual topics, for example *The Foot Book* and *Fitness After Forty.*

Kuntzleman, Charles T. *Activetics.* New York: Peter H. Wyden Co., 1975.

Not your usual running book, but a tremendous essay on weight control. Some of the concepts on body fat make this book worth having (including a way to estimate your own body fat — something most runners need to know). Highly recommended as another book for your shelf.

Kurpis, Bonnie Storch. *Easy Running.* New York: Dell Publishing Co., 1978.

Another general how-to book with very little that's new. It becomes more and more difficult to add spice to where to run, how to run, and when to run. About all the newer authors can do is contribute personal feelings about what the exercise means to them.

Lance, Kathryn. *Running for Health and Beauty: A Complete Guide for Women.* Indianapolis, Indiana: Bobbs-Merrill Co., 1977.

The title gives this away as another how-to book for the female runner. Ms. Lance provides the reader with the usual data on running and there's a solid section on dangers to women from the mugger.

Leonard, George. *The Ultimate Athlete.* New York: Avon Books, 1977.

A head-trip book about sport with running included. Author Leonard deals with harmonizing forces, the pain of competing, and the heightened awareness that seems to be prevalent among the top athletes. An interesting book that points up the dangers from pursuing running to the point of mania. The threshold where injuries occur is also examined.

Milvy, Paul, ed. *The Long Distance Runner: A Definitive Study.* New York: Urizen Books, 1978.

There's not much that can be said that hasn't been said

184

about running, yet more and more books show up all the time. This book, however, comes closest to the ultimate book on what running is all about. It's a collection of essays by famous running personalities: Dr. George Sheehan, Dr. Thaddeus Kostrubala, Dr. Steven Subotnick (the running foot doctor), Dr. Thomas Bassler (the provocative cardiologist who believes that marathoning builds absolute immunity to heart attacks), and many more.

If you're interested in all of the latest information on running — technical and nontechnical — this might be the only book you'll ever need on the subject. At the same time, there's a repetition that creeps into all the new literature based upon a reworking of the data already extant. An expensive book with a lot of information.

Mirkin, Gabe, and Hoffman, Marshall. *The Sports Medicine Book.* Boston: Little, Brown & Co., 1978.

An oversized book filled with information on injuries and the problems with exercise. Running is treated in a thorough fashion. A solid book for the beginner to read.

Myers, Clayton R. *The YMCA Physical Fitness Handbook.* New York: Popular Library, 1975.

A fine little book covering many aspects of cardiovascular exercise. Chapter 5 deals with ideal weight and has a valuable conversion formula for estimating body fat from waist size and the use of a scale.

Chapter 8 gives tests to determine fitness that don't stress the week-end warrior and deliver him up to the injury list. Inexpensive and worth putting on your shelf.

Olney, Ross R. *The Young Runner.* New York: William Morrow Co., 1978.

Another how-to book but aimed at the younger runner. Most of the information can apply to anyone taking up jogging as an exercise, though. However, young people do have special injury problems that are related to their age and propensity for working to exhaustion, so this is an especially valuable book for young joggers and their families.

Osler, Tom. *The Serious Runner's Handbook.* Mountain View, California: World Publications, 1978.

Another how-to book by a fine runner. The same kind of information that you'll find in the "complete" and "guide" books.

Proxmire, William. *You Can Do It!* New York: Simon & Schuster, 1975.

A "macho" approach to exercise by a famous senator.

He delivers his running testimonial with more than a hint of challenge. A book that should be read with an eye on the problems that Mr. Proxmire passes by in his unbridled enthusiasm. He has chapters on diet and other areas of health. The first chapter, entitled "Your Patriotic Duty," sets the tone for this book.

Rohe, Fred. *The Zen of Running.* New York: Random House, 1975.

The ultimate head-trip book. This oversized book is filled with pictures and text aimed at raising the runner's consciousness. The pictures are lovely, the text poetic in nature. This is certainly not a very practical book and gives the reader no indication of the problems associated with running. However, for sheer beauty, this book can't be matched.

Runner's World editors. *Beginning Running.* Mountain View, California: World Publications, 1972.

Another "booklet of the month" with thirty-two pages of information on how to get started jogging. Some very straightforward techniques are offered that can give the new runner a glimpse of what he's facing. On page 8 there's a prerun safety check that *recommends medical clearance for middle-aged newcomers.* Worth reading and a booklet that should be given to friends who are asking all the right questions.

Runner's World editors. *Runner's Training Guide.* Mountain View, California: World Publications, 1973.

Another splendid "booklet of the month" from *Runner's World* magazine. This collection includes articles on why someone should train, interpretations from the great coaches, and discussions of the various events from sprints through distances. This is a booklet for those who wish to move up from gentle jogging to the rigors of competitive racing. The injuries are played down and the runner is encouraged to get going.

Runner's World editors. *The Complete Runner.* New York: Avon Books, 1974.

Dated. A collection of articles on various aspects of running; a combination of morale-builder, head-trip, and the general how-to offering. Some of the information is helpful; however, even when injuries and definite hazards are pointed out for the reader, there's a certain positive drift that outweighs any warning. The book also contains the very dangerous fifteen-minute test that hasn't been cleared for the week-end runner.

Runner's World editors. *First Steps to Fitness.* Mountain View, California: World Publications, 1974.

One more in the series of booklets from *Runner's World* magazine introducing the new runner to a world of stretching, pacing, cardiovascular fitness, and all of the alleged benefits of jogging.

Runner's World editors. *New Exercise for Runners.* Mountain View, California: World Publications, 1978.

Bob Anderson, chief mentor of *Runner's World* magazine, has always been extremely interested in stretching exercises for runners. This book is the natural outgrowth of that interest. Stretching, as we have seen, can be the difference between years of painfree running and a career riddled with injuries. The muscular development of each runner is dependent upon a cohesive program of stretching, together with the proper amount of mileage. This release gives the runner a program of stretching based upon the latest techniques.

Shapiro, Jim. *On The Road: The Marathon.* New York: Crown Publishers, 1978.

If you liked *The Boston Marathon* by Joe Falls, you'll love this book too. Author Shapiro gives us all of the wacky and wonderful happenings that surround marathoning and points out the extent of this mania. Good reading and an excellent illustration of just how dangerous the run can be from a beginner's point of view.

Sheehan, George A. *Doctor Sheehan on Running.* Mountain View, California: World Publications, 1975.

This was the first of many successful Sheehan books. His formula — a little information, a lot of homespun philosophy — and a market ready for Dr. Sheehan.

Sheehan is one of those runners who writes as well as he competes. A cardiologist in New Jersey, Dr. Sheehan loves to quote Ortega y Gasset while telling us all about shin splints, electrolyte replacement, and how to have a quick bowel movement before the big marathon.

The good doctor's philosophy of life (and therefore his philosophy of running, since the two areas overlap for him), can be summed up by an Ortega quote he uses in the beginning of his book: "Life is a desperate struggle to succeed in being in fact that which we are in design."

One of the better morale-building books.

Sheehan, George A. *Doctor Sheehan's Medical Advice for Runners.* Mountain View, California: World Publications, 1978.

At last, a book on injuries. A book dedicated to the thousand and one questions that runners trying to adhere to an ambitious program have.

A natural result of Dr. Sheehan's medical advice column in *Runner's World* magazine, this book is a must for any runner sincerely interested in keeping whole as well as fit. The book speaks to every kind of injury from biomechanical problems to disease.

Sheehan, George A. *Running and Being: The Total Experience.* New York: Simon & Schuster, 1978.

This book picks up the philosophical Sheehan where he left off in *Doctor Sheehan on Running.* Again he tells us about the wonders of life and running as if the two are inseparable. If anyone qualifies for the unlikely term of running guru, Dr. George Sheehan does. Good reading for a cozy weekend.

Note: Sheehan's warnings on the runner's problems are there, but obscured by his genuine romance with CVE.

Spino, Mike. *Beyond Jogging: The Innerspaces of Running.* Millbrae, California: Celestial Arts, 1976.

A head-trip book that's in a class by itself. Mike Spino offers all kinds of information related to the "cerebral high" of running. If you're into the metaphysics of running (and I'm sure someone is busy writing such a book at the moment), Spino's trips will be interesting.

Running will never be the same after Spino. He is against the steady jog with little or no change in tempo. He feels it is not creative and is actually enervating. In place of this he offers the devotee an imaginative variety of tempos, styles and the idea of visualizing the kinds of things that make head-trips a reality.

Not much to complain about here — Spino, a physical fitness counselor, makes running into a dream.

Stiller, Richard. *Pain: Why it Hurts, Where it Hurts, When it Hurts.* Nashville, Tennessee: Thomas Nelson, 1975.

An interesting book on injuries. It seems to be well accepted now that any runner who runs through severe pain is asking for permanent disability. Pain is a symptom and requires investigation.

Subotnick, Steven I. *The Running Foot Doctor.* Mountain View, California: World Publications, 1977.

Another version of the *Foot Book* by a man who treats runners. This book not only explains the various kinds of injuries but identifies them through case histories. The various ways you can wrap a foot to prevent pressure from building up are worth the price of the book all by itself. A good one to have on your shelf.

Ullyot, Joan. *Women's Running*. Mountain View, California: World Publications, 1976.

A general how-to book aimed at women but applicable to everyone who runs. As with so many other books, this effort seems to be just another running book with a "once over lightly" for what ails you.

van Aaken, Ernst. *The van Aaken Method: Finding the Endurance to Run Faster and Live Healthier*. Mountain View, California: World Publications, 1976.

One of the true geniuses at coaching the runner. He has produced many top racers and continues to help runners despite the fact that he lost both legs in a collision with a motor vehicle in 1971.

Ziegel, Vic, and Grossberger, Lewis. *The Non-Runner's Guide*. New York: Collier Books, 1978.

I've added this one because it can be mistaken for a book against running. It isn't that at all, but a very funny composition that adds a new dimension to satire. When you open this book you're faced with a dedication to Calvin Coolidge who once said that he "chose not to run." Incidentally, the cover has an uncanny resemblance to *The Complete Book of Running* by Jim Fixx. The difference is that although the same beautiful red color is used, instead of Mr. Fixx's bulging calves staring at us from the cover we have a trash can with running artifacts unceremoniously strewn about. A charming book, but definitely not one that will enable the reader to find out what's wrong with running.

Magazines, local publications as well as the nationally known ones, fall into two categories: (1) the magazine that is technically oriented and seems to be an offshoot of the old physical education journals; and (2) the slick magazine that blends technical articles with biographical sketches and splashy stories, complete with stunning photos of runners circling tracks, crossing deserts and even climbing straight up mountains.

The magazines that follow are just a few of the dozens that are part of the running subculture's literature.

The Runner, New Times Publishing Company; monthly.

George A. Hirsch, *New Times* publisher, qualifies as a running nut. After advertising that this magazine would be for all levels of runners, he delivered what he promised. The first issue included articles about body fat, how to improve mileage, an article by Frank Shorter on training for speed, and a nifty biographical piece on Fritz Mueller, one of the top over-forty runners in the country.

What set *The Runner* apart was its style — easy reading, lots of fun, and very informative — brought to the magazine from the *New Times* staff. Weaknesses, many. First, running was most always portrayed as a kind of "in" sport for those with time, money and the opportunity to take off for exotic places to do their running. The average jogger may never climb Pike's Peak, or circle the beautiful Honolulu area, or cross numerous bridges on his way to a spectacular finish in the New York City Marathon. Yet what do we all do? Dream. And that's where *The Runner* answered the call.

Another issue highlighted stress tests, the number of political butterflies into running, profiles of the New York Marathon (publisher Hirsch's personal race) and marathoner Bill Rodgers (who just about owns the NYC race).

Interesting reading with technical articles scattered here and there.

Runner's World, World Publications; monthly.

Some runners would call this magazine out of Mountain View, California, the bible of cardiovascular exercise. This monthly offers articles that range from technical studies on the effects of air pollution on the typical neighborhood jogger to the food fads of Frank Shorter and Brian Maxwell.

Runner's World is one of the fastest growing specialty magazines in the country. The running explosion pushed subscriptions to an all-time high and moved a part-time publishing company into a small but still evolving publishing empire. More than half the books in the selected annotated bibliography come from the World Publications presses. Many times the books and booklets are longer versions of articles that have already appeared in the magazine. No serious runner could do without a monthly mail delivery including *Runner's World.*

One major feature that has grown over the years is the October issue devoted to analyzing and rating the running shoes produced in this country. It would seem that a high ranking in the annual shoe issue would just about guarantee a manufacurer that his brand of expensive foot covering would sell handily months after the list appeared, while a poor ranking might condemn the manufacturer. There's considerable evidence that the readership does rely on *Runner's World* for information concerning products.

Another very interesting issue arrives each May, with complete results, in-depth stories and lots of color from the great Boston Marathon. This magazine can't be surpassed for covering such a major running event.

Weaknesses? Yes. The magazine is slowly evolving into a technical journal. Many of the articles and features are aimed at the serious runner trying to make a name for himself at local meets. Some of the dangers are underrated and without Dr. Sheehan's column on medical advice a beginning runner might think the sport was without hazards.

One last warning: it seems to this writer that the issues have had a repetitive nature lately. Has *Runner's World* fallen into that major trap of producing a winning formula and then trying not to stray at all? The main problem with *Runner's World* is that it hasn't decided whether it will take its place as "the" technical journal on running or "the" pop-running magazine. Either way, the beginner has to read carefully and not become bored with the tremendous amount of big-time advertising.

Running, Salem, Oregon; quarterly.

You're thinking that since I live in Oregon, I'm naturally inclined to report on a local magazine. Wrong. *Running* happens to be one of the best technical journals around. Publisher Jack Welch doesn't provide the slick, somewhat pop flavoring that prevails in the previous two magazines listed. He prefers to report on the advantages and disadvantages of running. Equally important, the articles aren't too long or filled with color pictures that take away from the information. A current issue covered such diverse topics as the value of injuries, the different kinds of drinks that are used to help replace electrolytes, and the importance of understanding the functions of the running foot.

Today's Jogger, New York; monthly.

Beautiful people doing their thing — this is the way to describe the covers of *Today's Jogger.* A cross between *The Runner* and *Runner's World, Today's Jogger* doesn't have the expensive look nor the market appeal of the others. However it is making tracks and can be counted on to provide some interesting material (even if the pictures make it look as if only healthy people cavort in Central Park). A recent issue covered the ten most common jogging injuries and told how to prevent them, explained how to keep your feet reasonably healthy, gave easy warm-up exercises and advice on how to kick the habit of eating too much sugar. Plenty of sound advice here.

On The Run, World Publications; twice monthly.

Runner's World must have so much material left over each month that the excess can be recycled in the form of a tabloid newspaper twice a month. *On The Run* is a scaled down, inexpensive *Runner's World,* complete with the same type of articles, features, and naturally, advertising. Interesting reading but really an overlap with the monthly.

Marathoner, World Publications; quarterly.

A really slick magazine for the absolutely dedicated runner searching for a way to be part and parcel of the running community and its subculture. Lavishly illustrated with color pictures of runners feverishly attacking mountains, fording streams and generally tackling the marathons offered each year, *Marathoner* provides its readership with a kind of "dessert" to go along with the main course set out by other running magazines.

The following books, some not specifically on running but related to fitness and health, can provide added insights and help you decide if running is the type of exercise you wish to pursue.

Bailey, Covert. *Fit or Fat?* Boston: Houghton & Mifflin, 1978.

Blanda, George, with Mickey Herskowitz. *Over Forty: Feeling Great and Looking Good!* New York: Simon & Schuster, 1978.

Broom, Skip, and John Grahm. *Target 26.* London: Collier Macmillan Publishers, 1979.

Brunner, Daniel; Galton, Lawrence; and Miller, Benjamin. *Freedom from Heart Attacks.* New York: Simon & Schuster, 1978.

Fossbender, William. *You and Your Health.* New York: Wiley, 1977.

Franklin, Marshall; Krauthamer, Martin; and Tai, A. Razzak. *The Heart Doctor's Heart Book.* New York: Bantam Books, 1974.

Gallup, George, and Hill, Evan. *The Secrets of Long Life.* New York: Crown Publishing Co., 1959.

Hrachovec, Josef P. *Keeping Young & Living Longer.* Nashville, Tennessee: Sherbourne Press, 1972.

Kuntzleman, Charles T. and the editors of *Consumer Guide. Rating the Exercises.* New York: William Morrow and Co., 1978.

————. *The Exerciser's Handbook.* New York: David McKay, 1978.

Lathrop, Theodore G. *Hypothermia: Killer of the Unprepared.* Portland, Oregon: Mazamas, 1975.

Levetos, Irwin M., and Machal, Libby. *You Can Beat the Odds on a Heart Attack.* New York: Bobbs-Merrill, 1975.

Lilliefors, Jim. *Total Running: All About the Spiritual Side of Running.* New York: William Morrow & Co., 1979.

Steffny, Manfred. *Marathoning: A Book.* Mountain View, California: World Publishing Co., 1979.

Subotnick, Steven. *Cures for Common Running Injuries.* Mountain View, California: World Publishing Co., 1979.

We've reached the end of our selected and annotated bibliography, but the number of books and magazines continues to grow without end. Spend some time browsing in your local library or bookstore, using these suggestions as a launching pad, and then go on to explore the newer offerings. You'll find plenty of material whether you're a block-circler, a daily jogger or a marathoner. But remember — it's as important to read your own body and its capabilities and strengths (or weaknesses) as it is to read every running book on the market.

EPILOGUE

We've come a long way since tackling the running glow that's caught on around the country. We've looked at the who and what of running, the how of running, and even the why of hitting the streets. However, every inch of the way the same message came through: watch out, runners are in danger, and *running* can be *dangerous!*

We have emphasized *prevention* instead of recovery; *avoidance* in place of help later. An ounce of prevention, the cliche goes, is worth a pound of cure, and in running, this is true. A small amount of common sense is worth much more than enthusiasm that blinds the exerciser. It's more difficult to heal a torn Achilles tendon than to *prevent* the tear in the first place.

Why does this message seem difficult to put over? Why,

indeed! The importance of running safely and sanely must be fostered by the joggers themselves. If we don't do it, who will? If we don't press the running subculture for a more realistic attitude toward sudden exercise deaths, who will? And if we who love to run don't practice what we preach, just who will?

It comes down to a social conscience. It's time for the running community to cease putting commercial values ahead of human values, to stop *selling* running as if it were snake oil, to respect it as the potent (and potentially lethal) force it is.

The time is now!

APPENDIX

Oregon Road Runners Club Survey

The results of this survey were based on 100 runners from the large and popular Oregon Road Runners Club. All the runners sampled had these common characteristics: (1) Male; (2) 35 to 60 years of age; and (3) active runners as of July, 1977. The very high percentage who returned the questionnaire (80 per cent) indicates that runners enjoy talking about themselves!

Average number of miles run per day:	5.0
Length of time jogging:	4.1 years
Age at time of questionnaire:	44.4 years
Reason for beginning running program:	
Fitness:	71.1%
Weight control:	11.1%
Continued from school:	11.1%
Friend's advice:	6.7%*

*This category includes information from books and magazines.

Do you believe that jogging does any of the following? (multiple response included):

Provides overall better state of health:	21.6%
Prevents heart disease:	21.0%
Extends life by retarding aging:	17.9%
Helps control weight:	15.4%
Improves quality of life:	6.8%
Improves mental outlook:	6.2%
Reduces stress:	5.6%
Prevents some types of cancers:	4.3%
Prevents most illness:	1.2%

Did you suffer any bothersome injuries related directly to running?

Yes:	70.8%
No:	29.2%

Types of injuries:

Feet:	41.5%
Legs:	39.6%
Knees:	11.3%
Back:	7.5%

Did you incur any lung or heart problems from jogging?

Yes:	2.1%
No:	97.9%

Did you take a stress test before or during the jogging program?

Yes:	16.7%
No:	83.3%

For the 16.7% who had a stress test, was it updated?

Yes:	37.5%
No:	62.5%

Longest continuous run in workout or competition (average for the group responding): 21 miles

Warmest temperature during jogging (average for the group responding): 93.6° F.

Coldest temperature during jogging (average for the group responding): 10.0° F.

What are the dangers in jogging?

Running without a warm-up:	33.7%
Running too far, too soon:	32.6%
Training with too much strain:	14.6%
Not having the right shoes:	12.4%
Irregular program:	4.5%
Downhill running stress:	2.2%

What are the benefits for newcomers?

Fitness improvement:	48.3%
Improved mental outlook:	38.3%
Weight control:	8.3%
Achievement factors:	5.0%

Number of joggers in the family (average for the group responding): 1.9 persons

The survey is interesting from the point of view that most of the runners responding to the questionnaire indicated that they were not "fooling around" with their running program. (Granted that a member of a running club is probably more inclined toward heavy workouts and racing, still there are many events the club sponsors that do not take the kind of dedication shown by the survey.)

Another interesting point is that the running programs of these middle-aged joggers, few of whom had taken a stress test before they began running, were quite ambitious, averaging five miles a day for four years. Moreover, and something to think about, over 70 per cent were bothered with injuries related to running — seven out of every ten respondents!

The respondents were also accustomed to some fairly extreme weather. The averages for hot and cold fall within the danger zones outlined in this book. Also, the runners believe that their heavy schedules, regardless of injuries and dangers to their bodies, can do many wonderful things for them (including those who believe it prevents most illnesses — even cancer!).

—